# LUTON SIXTH FORM COLLEGE

### BRADGERS HILL ROAD
### LUTON BEDS
### LU2 7EW

**Return on or before the last date stamped below.**

# People Make Plays

## Aspects of Community Theatre in Hull since 1955

Editor
### Pamela Dellar

Foreword by
### Richard Hoggart

Highgate Publications (Beverley) Ltd.
1992

© Copyright Individual Contributors 1992

Cataloguing in Publication
Data Available

ISBN 0 948929 61 8

Published by Highgate Publications (Beverley) Ltd.
24 Wylies Road, Beverley, HU17 7AP.
Telephone (0482) 866826

Printed and Typeset in 10 on 11 Plantin by
Colourspec, Unit 7, Tokenspire Park,
Hull Road, Woodmansey, Beverley, HU17 0TB.
Telephone (0482) 864264

*Front Cover:*
*The Company of the Way in* The Sport of My Mad Mother *by Anne Jellicoe. Directed by Tony Wharmby, 1964. Photograph taken outside St. Mary's Church, Lowgate, Hull.*

*Photograph by courtesy of the* Hull Daily Mail

# CONTENTS

*Frontispiece by John Munday from the programme for his production of the* Noah Play, *1977.*

# CONTRIBUTORS

**Muriel Crane** took an M.A. with Honours in English at Edinburgh and had a spell with the Lyceum there before her appointment in 1946 as lecturer in literature and drama in the Adult Education Department at Hull University. She spent summers with rep theatres at Bristol, Windsor and Bradford, and studied with Laban to learn more of practical theatre. In 1969 and 1975 she received Polish Government scholarships to study theatre there. She has served on various seminars run by I.T.I. and UNESCO on theatre, was external adviser to the Drama Panel of the Arts Council and member of the G.D.A. She retired in 1982.

**Rupert Creed** came to Hull in 1974 to study Drama and German at Hull University where he graduated with first class honours. In 1978 he started working for Hull Truck Theatre Company, first as stage manager and then as assistant director. With Averil Coult he founded Remould Theatre Company in 1981 and has written and directed 15 plays for the company. His other main interests apart from theatre are mountaineering and rock climbing.

**Pamela Dellar** (Editor) trained for the theatre in post-war London at the Central School of Speech and Drama. She worked in the professional theatre for eight years before coming to Hull in 1954 with her husband, Harold Dellar, who lectured at the University in Social Administration until his death in 1981. She helped found Hull Arts Centre/Spring Street Theatre and was the founder and professional director of Outreach Community Arts. Her book, *Plays Without Theatres,* was published in 1989 by Highgate Publications.

**Jennie Foreman** is now Head of Drama and Arts Organiser at Newland High School for Girls, Hull. She graduated from Hull University in English and Drama in 1970 and then studied at the Laban Movement Centre. This was followed by extensive work in the professional theatre, including Greenwich Theatre in Education. Her mask workshops for the Arts in School Project of the National Curriculum Council have been widely appreciated in recent years.

**Richard Green** was born in Hull. At the age of 13 he went to the Corona Stage School in London and then worked for a season with the Shakespeare Theatre Company at Stratford. This was followed by a season at Birmingham Rep. and tours with several Arts Council productions. He became disillusioned with the commercial theatre, took his L.R.A.M. and trained as a teacher in Hull. He is the founder of the Northern Theatre Company and is now Head of Drama at Wyke Sixth Form College.

**Jane Thomas** came to Hull in 1973 to study English at the University. In 1977 she began teaching at Hull College of Further Education while studying for her doctorate. Shortly before completing her Ph.D. she joined Hull Truck Theatre Company as their Community Theatre and Education Officer, leaving in 1989 to teach English part-time at Hull University. She now teaches English full-time at Bretton Hall College, Wakefield, and is writing a critical book on Thomas Hardy's novels which will be published by Macmillan.

**Ron Walker** lived in Hull all his life before moving to Stonecroft House Cheshire Home at Barnetby on the Wolds. His disability, cerebral palsy, has not prevented him from being actively involved in drama and the folk scene in Hull over the years. He is an executive member of Artlink Management Committee and a founder member of Hull Disability Arts Forum. He has recently returned to Hull so that he can be more closely involved in re-establishing a theatre company for disabled people.

**J. Michael Walton** is Reader in Theatre History in Hull University Drama Department. He attended the Universities of St. Andrews and Bristol before gaining an Independent Television (ABC) Trainee Director's Award to spend a year at the Theatre Royal, York, where he acted and directed in 1965. He is the author of several books on Greek Theatre and General Editor of Methuen Classical Texts in Translation. He has been Visiting Professor at the University of Denver and Louisiana State University.

**Richard Hoggart,** who has kindly written our foreword for us, was a member of the staff of Hull University's Extramural Department for 13 years from 1946 during which time he completed and published *The Uses Of Literacy*, his seminal study of working class life. He became Professor of Modern English Literature at Birmingham and founded there The Centre for Cultural Studies. From there he went to Paris as UNESCO'S Assistant Director General for five years. He then became Warden of Goldsmith's College until 1984. The final volume of his autobiographical trilogy, *An Imagined Life*, was published earlier this year by Chatto and Windus.

# FOREWORD

If you live in Hull, you soon learn to ignore the stale jokes about the place. An isolated medium-sized city, separated by more than fifty miles of largely agricultural land from the main rail and road communications-spine of Britain and with little else but semi-rural land, sea and river in other directions. Such a place is bound to seem, to be assumed to be, dull and somnolent to those who live in the great metropolitan clusters.

But Hull and its residents need neither patronage nor pity. It is a fresh and healthy town, comely in many of its aspects, with a fine mediaeval centre, a wonderful expanse of busy waterway and a haunting hinterland. A fine town to bring up a family in, a liveable town; and with far more happening week by week than a coastal visitor would expect.

In particular it has been, in forty or so more years from the end of the war to the late Eighties, one of the liveliest and most productive cities in Britain for dramatic work, amateur and professional. It is part of this record which the present book describes and, with becoming modesty, celebrates.

Too many people are mentioned in these essays to make it proper to name any of them. But one of the first great inspirers has been dead for a dozen years and can reasonably be named.

G. E. T. Mayfield became Professor of Adult Education at the University College (as it was then) immediately after the war. His great love was literature and, within that, drama. Undeterred by the Ministry of Education's refusal to fund the practice of drama as compared with the classroom study of drama, he appointed a number of clever and dedicated young tutors who went out into the City and the Riding and over into Lincolnshire to promote both study and practice. That was the first flowering of what became a sustained town-and-gown interaction. It was followed in the early Sixties by the acceptance of Drama, theoretic and practical, as a subject for internal study by the University and, fairly soon since that was an expansive decade, by the establishment of a full Department there.

The first free-standing drama group to come out of those years was the Company of the Way, founded in 1955. Many others followed in the Fifties, Sixties, Seventies and Eighties: theatre for children, for the disabled, for the cause of feminism, for special community work, for experimental projects and so on. One of the main impressions from a reading of all this is of the readiness to be inventive, to range very widely indeed in themes and approaches and in the audience sought. With that goes admiration for the vast amount of time and energy, of devotion of all kinds, which so many people with different gifts put at the disposal of their chosen groups.

A great number of local institutions played their parts too: the Local Authority, the College of Technology, of Art and of Higher Education; and a range of voluntary bodies who were brought to see how the practice of drama, as well as being interesting in itself, could link with their own briefs.

It is not fanciful to suspect that the manifold dramatic activities of places such as Hull (though there were not many such places) helped the Arts Council, when its funds began to be greatly increased in the Sixties, to understand better what the needs of the provinces were, what was due to places which can seem, from Piccadilly, like blank spots in a large and somewhat empty hinterland. The Arts Council is forbidden to support amateur activity. But in the Sixties and Seventies it established a network of professional theatres right across the country. The dramatic activity of places such as Hull helped them to see that there were audiences out there who wanted more and could appreciate more than they had so far been given from the metropolis. No doubt some universities, of which Hull was one of the earliest, were helped on to the recognition of the claims of drama by the same evidence. As was the Gulbenkian Foundation, a most artistically-imaginative sponsor in those decades.

Later on, Hull's strength in professional theatre — with Alan Plater living in the town, with John Godber and Hull Truck, and with Remould Theatre Company — seemed not fortuitous but in some subtle cultural way connected with all that had gone before, in amateur no less than in professional activity.

Drama in Hull today is by no means dead. But the effervescence was bound to subside in the mid-Eighties. Money was becoming tighter and tighter from the mid-Seventies onwards: in the universities, in local government and in arts-funding bodies. some painful decisions had to be taken by all those and, inevitably, the best decisions were not always made. At such times, the arts begin to seem, once again and as is habitual in Britain, a luxury we can hardly afford. The arts rarely have seats in the committee rooms of power.

Yet it would be wrong to end on a depressing note. The Eighties have been a bad time for all activities which insist that we do not live by bread alone. The battle has to be fought in each generation and will go on being fought, in Hull as elsewhere. The Hull example is a very good one and will provide a fine launching-pad for the next surge upwards.

RICHARD HOGGART

# INTRODUCTION

In 1989 I set myself the task of preparing a book about the development of post-war theatre in Hull and invited the people I knew had been involved in this to contribute. I should have known, of course, that there would be far too much material for just one book because over more than three decades the growth has increased enormously.

Perhaps it was a coincidence that the first contributions to come in were from those who have been concerned with widening access to drama and the arts especially through further and higher education, and continuing and informal education. The co-operation of Hull University Department of Adult Education in publishing these essays in collaboration with Highgate Publications helped to confirm the decision to publish them separately. But the next book is already in preparation and will tell the story of the development of the amateur theatre in the city and its relationship to the professional theatre.

At present (1991/2) a nationwide debate is in progress, established in 1990 and headed by the National Arts and Media Strategy Unit of the Arts Council. It acknowledges that demand has grown for access to the arts. Public and private resources have struggled to keep up. What should the priorities be?. Such decisions have to be based on firm evidence. I hope the experiences we tell of opening up the barricades in one fairly small, isolated city will help to illustrate the need expressed by many people for the opportunity to be involved in the arts at all levels and in all ways.

In 1992 the future for theatre and the performing arts in Hull looks bright. This is in large part due to the work which is being done in the schools and through the youth theatre groups.

In addition the Humberside Theatre in Education provides a free service to Humberside schools. It developed through the work of John Marshall and Jenny Duffin at Humberside Theatre (now Spring Street Theatre) in the 1970's and was finally established in 1983.

As this book will show, there have been many struggles and setbacks over the years; but now, with such a wide spectrum of events for young people, we can all look forward to the lively and informed arts scene that is appearing in Hull in the last decade of the twentieth century.

Finally, I would like to thank all the people who have contributed to this book: both the writers and the participants in all the activities described.

Also Alan Davis, Richard Penton, the *Hull Daily Mail*, Dave Whatt, Donald Hawkins for permission to reproduce their photographs. Special thanks are due to Wendy Munday for permission to print John Munday's designs and drawings — this is a special tribute to him for all he did for community theatre before his death in 1991. I would like to add a tribute to Lesley Scarr for her community theatre work before illness forced her to retire. My deep gratitude goes to Dr. Elfrede Bickersteth for her generous help and to James Deighton for the cover design. Also to Rosa Brown, Jayne Chatterton and the staff of Hull University Adult Education Department and to John Markham, Irene and Martin Kirby of Highgate Publications and Barry Sage of Colourspec.

PAMELA DELLAR

# CHAPTER ONE

# NEW SCRIPTS, STYLES AND SPACES

## The Company of the Way, 1955-70
## Hull University Adult Education Department Theatre Workshop 1970-78

### by Muriel Crane

My contribution to this account of theatre in Hull post-war has two parts. The first part deals with the Company of the Way, a religious drama group formed by Frank and Frances Glendenning and myself in 1955. The second part is about the class known as Theatre Workshop run by the Department of Adult Education at the University between 1970 and 1978. The projects reflect what was going on nationally in theatre in that period, the exciting new plays, the hope that every city would have its art centre, the need to develop new styles of acting and training, new ways of staging plays. They obviously connect with my commitment to the Department's policy of providing tutors and classes in theatre appreciation and practice throughout the area, a policy originated by Professor G. E. T. Mayfield who appointed me and other full-time lecturers in drama and literature. Theatre Workshop grew out of The Company of the Way and the work of many remarkable people associated with it.

When Frank Glendenning came to Hull in 1955 to be Anglican chaplain at the University and Vicar of St. Mary's, Lowgate, in Hull, he and his wife Frances brought with them the idea of making the ancient church in the middle of Hull's business and commercial old town into a base for an 'arts in the city' project. He contacted me. I had just opted out of full-time work for the University to look after a young family, so I was delighted to collaborate as director with Frank, free of the travel and preparation that extramural teaching involves. The Glendennings also drew in others with specialist knowledge, like John Joubert, lecturer and composer in the University Music Department, Nancy Lamplugh, lecturer in Dress and Textiles at the regional College of Art (as it was then), George Pace, the architect and consultant to Llandaff, Sheffield, Durham and other cathedrals. Frank had a University lecturer in theology, John Tinsley (later Bishop of Bristol), assisting him at Lowgate, and John's special enthusiasm for the visual arts ensured that he gladly joined the fellowship. This isn't the place to do justice to all the cultural achievements of those three years when the best musicians in the area played concerts of Palaestrina, Tallis or Haydn's *Seven Last Words*, the most creative craftspeople exhibited designs for church artefacts, vestments and so on, showing these need not be banalities turned out wholesale. Art wasn't to be remote and rarified.

The Company of the Way, as its name indicates, developed its own identity and survived beyond the three years in which the achievements of the arts experiment in the city flourished. While Frank and Frances were in Hull they were passionately involved in the drama side. Frank was a good actor with splendid voice and technical assurance. Frances too was willing to act or to serve the plays in any practical way. As her essay, *Drama Theatre and Church*, shows, she admired the work then being done by the Religious Drama Society and by the touring Pilgrim Players. Frank collected essays from us all in *The Church and The Arts* ed. Frank Glendenning, S.C.M. 1960. This was a handful of actors with the simplest costumes, properties and lighting, who brought the best of the verse drama by Eliot, Fry, Ridler and Nicholson to the towns and villages. Until '1956 and all that' these verse dramatists were seen as the theatre's phoenixes risen from the ashes, not just of the war but also of the burnt out commercial theatre of the 20s to 50s, offering mainly 'repeat prescriptions'. Frances Glendenning was a gentle academic with considerable knowledge of and love for the theatre. We all three wanted to present the best drama in the best way. There was no virtue in putting on parish pump homilies when our specialists in music and the visual arts were engaged with Palaestrina, Tallis and *Haydn's Seven Last Words* or exhibitions of architectural and textile design, displays of new craftspeople's work. We wanted to present the best religious plays past or contemporary and to set up a group that would achieve distinction based on talent (naturally) but above all on the hard work in rehearsals that would involve training in voice and movement where necessary, plus the creation of a good back stage team.

We brought together amateurs from about 20 different parishes, mainly Anglican, although our policy was to be ecumenical. Our first programme consisted of two contrasting plays. The medieval Hull play of *Noah* (which the Shipwrights' Guild used to perform in the Corpus Christi Day Festivals) we performed in the churchyard of St. Mary's. The other play was Yeats' *Resurrection*, played inside the church, as the piece we felt suited the shadowy interior of the City church. We had a lengthy rehearsal period in the upstairs parish room, which was icy in the winter and spring of 1955-6. Our cast had to take the trouble to come into or back into the City after their day's work, usually by public transport (cheap and plentiful then fortunately). They accepted a strenuous rehearsal discipline since artistic excellence calls for willing learning, sustaining attention over long periods, taxing the memory, observation and imagination. It taxes one physically as

2

well. But the amateur has time on his/her side, something the professional has not, especially in the under-subsidised theatre of today. To help a cast understand the text, to use improvisation when it helps, to teach techniques to inexperienced players, to ensure props are used dramatically, costumes ready to be worn early, to reach a standard of fluency that has the right rhythms and inflections, both in voice and in movement, and above all to build an ensemble, all require generous rehearsal time.

For *Noah* we had to have sets and props early to rehearse the ark building sequence for which I invented a kind of ballet. In this we were lucky to have Oliver Webb of the Garrett Players who was ingenious and reliable. Gill Holtby had just returned to Hull after a spell in repertory and she joined us, which added invaluable and various resources to our team, as anyone who has worked with or for her will know. She was able to provide skilled make-up, fine props, design costumes, organise the making of them, and in later shows she was a joy to have in a cast for her elegant and intelligent acting.

The performances were in July and, since *Noah*, would be played outdoors I used to phone up Leconfield R.A.F. Station for a daily weather forecast. The 'duty' boffin got quite involved in our enterprise and on that Friday he warned me of a stormy evening. It did pour down that evening but the timing was perfect. As Noah and crew prepared to set sail there was a growl from above and a few heavy raindrops fell. Then a crescendo of heavenly effects and it tippled down. Umbrellas were lifted, the cast offered to restart later but a fair number of spectators were game to continue and in the event the storm passed over. There were other hazards. In those days 'effects' had to be live or off records, since tape recorders were rare and beyond our means. I had found Bartok's *Roumanian Folk Dances* played at 45 instead of 78 (it was an old disc) suited the movement sequence for the building of the ark. I recall the anguish on the face of our music-man John Joubert as he watched me drop the needle onto chalk mark on the record. Then he heard Bartok at half speed and it took him a few moments to recover. We also got used to the passing drunk on Lowgate who would stop in amazement at the churchyard 'jolly', utter a few loud but friendly words and sometimes sit on the wall. We had not heard of 'street theatre' then.

After *Noah* the audience were ushered into the church where a fine trio of musicians (the Tunnicliffes and Marjorie Matthews) were playing Orlando Gibbons. Then came the Yeats' *Resurrection* played by Frank Glendenning, Ted Tilley and Geoffrey Hyder. The language imposed a ritualist style that also suited the church interior with its light and shadow, stained glass and fine carving. Like all churches it has blind spots, awkward sight lines, but it retains enough of the medieval sense of mystery to match Yeats' hieratic drama. I still remember the climax when the Christ Figure is seen returning to the upper room to seek the disciples, a moment intensified by John Joubert's setting of the songs to a score with a Byzantine-like percussion accompaniment. By the end of the week word of

3

mouth saw that we were packed out. The civic and academic presence of the great and the good encouraged us almost as much as the press notices did.

Our next venture originated in celebration of the 1300th anniversary of the founding of Whitby Abbey. The playwright James Kirkup whom I'd recently met at a departmental drama summer school was commissioned by Michael Ramsay, the Archbishop of York, to write a play for us. This was the kind of patronage for new works that Frank Glendenning hoped we could offer, not only for drama but also for music, and all the other arts represented by the Lowgate project. To encourage new works costs money and we were usually strapped for cash. I was sorry to have to 'sit this one out' when out two sons went down with suspected polio (it was the 'sugar-lump' time). But I had discussed briefly with James his draft of *Candle in the Heavens* and knew the poetry caught the spirit of Abbess Hilda's place and time, its imagery and rhythms evoking Streoneshalh or 'the place of light' as Whitby was known in Anglo-Saxon. One could visualise the limestone cliffs, the sea in all its moods, and the small community which was known throughout Europe for its learning and creativity.

James Kirkup followed the form of other Christian verse dramas of the period, and he wrote for a Chorus of Women of Whitby, which meant that our actresses had a decent share of the action as well as having language that was pleasurable to work on and to perform. Pamela Dellar had joined the Company by this time and she choreographed the movement of the chorus. Thus began her ten-year association with the Company as actor and Company secretary. Again John Joubert wrote music for us, a generous act that indicates his belief in work we were doing. Another gifted member of the team was Nancy Lamplugh who designed and supervised the making of the splendid costumes. As Frank writes, 'We felt it was a real meeting of the arts ... verbal, visual, mimetic and musical, a joint creation.' We performed it at four diocesan centres that summer, including one open-air performance at the Retreat House at Ryedale.

In retrospect I realise that *Candle in the Heavens* could only succeed in this particular setting and for this occasion. It was very much a study drama otherwise and has not since been performed. Our next choice was to me more exciting, even if I was still not directly involved. The Company presented T. S. Eliot's *Sweeney Agonistes*, an experimental fragment rarely freed from the page, although in it Eliot.uses demotic speech and jazz rhythms in a dynamic way that doesn't happen in his 'high society talkabout' pieces. The characters in *Sweeney* are tarts, hoods and Sweeney himself, a travesty of Milton's Samson. Of course it is only the briefest excursion into the surreal. Along with it the Company presented Gabriel Marcel's *Funeral Pyre*, a rather fey Christian existentialist piece. This bill was acted in the old assembly hall of the University and both plays were presented with inventiveness and panache. But the plays themselves raised questions in my mind. Were we restricting ourselves by choosing plays

4

which were by Christian playwrights only, when by 1956 a theatre renaissance offered a greater range of work reflecting our public and private realities in ways appropriate to our times?.

In 1959 the Glendennings had to leave Hull for Frank to take up his appointment as Warden at S.C.M. House in London. He was later to give up his vocation in the church and become secretary to Keele's Department of Adult Education under Roy Shaw (later Secretary General to the Arts Council). So the idea of the arts centre at St. Mary's ran out of steam, which demonstrates how much Frank and Frances were the generating power of the project. But the Company of the Way did continue, although not solely as a religious drama group. I had by 1960 returned on a half-time basis to my appointment as lecturer in drama and literature in the Department of Adult Education. So I was once more working extramurally taking classes all over the area, from York to Grimsby, Hull to Selby, and many classes in ·between. Our policy under 'Billy' Mayfield was to 'develop and encourage the practice and appreciation of drama in all its aspects within the University's extramural region'. My colleagues in drama were John Styan, Wilhelm Marckwald and Brian Clark. What with summer schools, day and weekend schools in addition to regular weekly classes, one works unsociable hours in adult education. But the Company of the Way was highly thought of by both Mayfield and Professor Styler who succeeded him. Moreover, we had built up a nucleus of fine performers and theatre crew keen to press on and willing to tackle unusual plays.

This is how we came to do Strindberg's *Easter* in 1959 at St. Margaret's Church in Spring Street. This rather derelict area was later to become the site of the Spring Street Arts Centre. *Easter* is a play which presents a moving story of the Heyst family's suffering, a parable of the unpredictable nature of all human suffering and redemption which Strindberg sets within the framework of Maundy Thursday to Easter Eve in a small Swedish 19th-century town. Its naturalistic surface is undercut by fantasy and the arbitrariness of characters and plot. It packs a powerful stage punch and the gloom is interspersed with lyricism and humour.

Pamela Dellar played the part of the scapegoat Eleanor whose 'madness' burdens her with intense empathy for the pain of others and whose unswerving faith brings her serenity but also agony in her fear of retribution. She soon accepted its fairy tale simplicity and gave the emotional subtext a remarkable power: her ability to sustain unbroken concentration and her complete identification with a role are amongst her gifts as an actress. We were lucky to have the late Harry Roach, headmaster of Hymers College, as Lindkvist, the dreaded creditor who turns out to be the agent of love and forgiveness. Harry would protest mildly from time to time that he really couldn't make sense of it all. Since he was a rationalist and classical scholar this wasn't surprising, but he had commanding physical presence on the stage and his own 'gentle giant' personality served the ogre archetype perfectly. He said to me he grew to enjoy being the one who 'brought the thing to a jolly end'. The parish hall platform was incidentally too shallow to project the huge shadow of Lindkvist into our back cloth effectively. I used to dread this moment until I realised that the cast who also knew the problem seemed to intensify their characters' panic superbly and the scene succeeded in spite of the deficiencies of the effect. The smallness and shallowness of the stage meant that the acting required a mastery of effective movement, gesture, and clean grouping, all the 'mechanics' of stage technique. Apart from Pam, the cast were fairly raw and needed detailed tuition in basics like sitting, handling a prop, holding silences, making economic moves and gestures without losing the illusion of ordinary behaviour on stage.

By now I was less happy about our doing only religious drama. In my own classes I was concerned not only with past masters but with contemporary theatre post-Samuel Beckett and Osborne, writing which expressed our age of uncertainty and alienation. Other concerns in classes were the new ideas about staging in the round or end-wise, any flexible and intimate disposition of actors and spectators which created the charged interaction which comes of both sharing the same space and being near enough to each other to avoid that cut-off of power when the actor's face is reduced to fingernail size. The new plays and the new kinds of auditoria needed fresh approaches to the art of acting. All this formed the content of my drama work and we were running a variety of short courses for amateur actors and directors to encourage them to be adventurous in choice and presentation. While I loved doing *Easter*, and its reception proved the virtue of daring to do the exotic or difficult, it was becoming hard to take on such demanding spare-time commitments as well as teach and travel widely for the Department. Professor Mayfield did arrange for the Company of the Way to give another performance of *Easter* at the University in the autumn.

In 1960 the company turned to touring plays. Our first venture was orthodox enough, being an adaptation of the medieval Cornish play of the *Three Maries*. We spoke it in local accents (more or less) to recover the vigour of folk speech and we persuaded one of the theology lecturers to play Christ. Unlike Frank Glendenning, Patrick Thompson was the most unactorish person you can imagine. He was a polymath with a saintly face, very tall and very thin. Beyond his shyness he had a nice wit and was very modest. This humility extended to acting, in which he wanted to give satisfaction but didn't know how. He asked me if he could do it numbers: 'One: I draw myself upright. Two: I raise my arms horizontal. Three: I speak one line. Four: I move my arms towards John and the girls ...' and so on. His wife Natasha told me he used to do it all *adagio* at the wardrobe mirror before rehearsals. His performance was a sensation and he had to shake off requests for more frequent stage appearances. I played Mary the Mother in this. As with all such tours, one has to sus out each new venue and adapt a basic plan whether in an old church like St. Mary's in Cottingham or a newer one like St. James' on Anlaby Road. The audiences were not on the whole accustomed to theatre-going and then there was a custom of not clapping in the church. But we appreciated the enthusiasm of those who did thank and entertain us, especially the enterprising priests and ministers who took up our offer.

Then we broke away from any religious content with a juvenile and jolly piece by young Roland Alan (later (aka) Alan Ayckbourn). This Christmas fantasy-comedy we took to some villages as well as doing a short run in Hull and Beverley. It also went down well at Pocklington School. It contains some robust farce, comic removal men and a gang of fairies whom he calls 'the tinies'. The cast included most of the regular members: Mary Bryan, Donald Campbell, Arthur Winstanley, Margot Blanchard, Pam Dellar, Freda Hobson, Jean Cox, Susie Robinson, Jack and Elma Ray, Bertram Wood and Gill Holtby. Then we could always bring in others when needed. I think it was about here that Frank Harris-Jones came to the University Registrar's Office and joined us to play many 'big' roles.

In 1962 we started a new phase in the story of the Company of the Way by doing the first amateur production of Pinter's *Birthday Party*. I wrote for his permission but got no reply. Rehearsals went on, however, and on the morning of the dress rehearsal Pinter's answer came: it was 'yes'! I'm not sure whether he would have liked my version, though. I made the 'grilling' scenes stylized in movement and gestures, whereas I've read that Pinter prefers a naturalist style. He handles language 'with sugar tongs', it's also been said, and the cast enjoyed the dialogue's mix of demotic and rhetorical. The menace and violence in the characters' situation and language split our audience into pro and anti functions. I don't think the outrage felt by the pre-war generation of playgoers when confronted by these iconoclastic new writers can be imagined today. We have so few taboos left.

We now reached 1963 and I realise that I cannot deal with every Company of the Way production in such detail. I will just give an honourable mention to the double bill we toured, although one of these, Albee's *American Dream*, won the Scarborough 'in the round' festival and Pam Dellar got a well deserved outstanding performer award. It was a strong cast, with Gill Holtby and Arthur Winstanley as Mommy and Daddy. The play we put with it was Alan Plater's *The Mating Season*, an ideal companion piece which also went well into the round, although the living room and the bedroom furniture needed a lot of man and woman handling, which is awkward when you are touring.

The next major production was a herculean undertaking, Ben Jonson's *Alchemist*. It had a cast of 19, an army of costumes makers carrying out Gill Holtby's designs, and 14 back-stage workers. Mary Bryan organised publicity, and front of house and we did it in the old assembly hall of the University. This proved a problem since the floor was unraked and our end staging against screens decorated with almebics, retorts and other motifs of the alchemical business was barely visible beyond the first few rows, even though seats were staggered. For all of us the most difficult task proved to be learning Jonson's lines. They lack the familiar rhythms and visuals of Shakespeare. Jonson's rhetoric has to go at a lick, yet be clearly heard by a modern audience unused to his splendid vulgarity, his ear for the language of London, and its canting inventiveness. Added to this are his scholarly allusions, parodies and the bizarre speech idioms that match each of his grotesques. Rehearsals foundered more than usually on memory lapses and the consequent frustrating losses of temper, of verve and confidence. It says a lot for this cast that they mastered the rhetoric and speed required of the style. They gave performances that concealed the huge input of physical and intellectual energy needed and achieved real virtuosity. The trio of rogues were played by Pamela Dellar (Doll Common), Frank Harris-Jones (Face) and Peter Redford (Subtle). Sir Epicure Mammon was lusciously presented by Mike Stephenson, and like the others mentioned he loved the language. I have happy memories of Don Roy's Sullen too.

Chance took us in an unforeseen direction in 1965. We were offered the use of a big ground floor room to be an arts centre. Our benefactors were Louise and Desmond Donovan and the room, which had its own outside entrance and lobby, was part of their Georgian house in Keldgate, Beverley. It had been an elegant music room in the 18th century but was now dirty and neglected. Many people caught our enthusiasm for the project and we spent days and evenings scrubbing floors and walls. Denis Simms gave us his professional expertise and redecorated the whole in its original Georgian colours. From January to July we worked to devise a programme of events including art exhibitions and visits from members of companies playing at the New Theatre, Hull. Alan Plater presented a programme of his own writing and so did Henry Livings and Alex Glasgow. We presented a programme of new writing based on the radio programme *Northern Drift* and later we staged a production of John Arden's *Ars Longa Vita Brevis*, in which half-masks featured. Arden himself was in the area for a drama weekend at Cober Hill and he came to one performance which he praised. There were snags at the Keldgate Centre: like limited space for parking and the only access to the lavatories being through the living quarters of the hospitable Donovan family. I don't think we would have got a general performance licence and we depended entirely on the generosity of our landlords. Then Professor Donovan was appointed to a chair of geology in London and the whole house was up for sale. His successor was one of my own colleagues in the Adult Education Department who, not surprisingly, preferred to put his extensive library in 'our' beautiful salon. We heard he liked the décor.

After this the centre of our activity became the University with all the advantages this offered. The Drama Department technicians often helped in many ways, we were able to use an old wooden gym called the theatre lab, and we could have the new Middleton Hall free. All this depended on my being 'staff', and the Company of the Way was at first an unofficial branch of the Adult Education programme. While Professor 'Bill' Styler encouraged this and helped in things like programmes or publicity, once I became full-time in 1970 we had to make the activity official. The Department of Education and Science does not subsidise cultural ventures as such and they had to be assured that its educational input was explicitly programmed and the resultant classes open to the public. These technicalities were more than formal, and I was just very glad that what the Company of the Way stood for was recognised and valued enough to be part of our adult programme. Two other experiences influenced the methods I used with Theatre Workshop classes. In 1967 I had spent a month with the R.S.C. attending rehearsals and going to Michel St. Denis' classes for the actors. The other formative experience was my three-month study of theatre in Poland in 1969 with another follow-up visit of a month in 1975. I went on a Polish government scholarship and they arranged a fortnight in Wroclaw at the contemporary theatre festival, free access to any rehearsals and shows all over the country, interviews with directors, attendance at conservatories and conferences. We conversed in French mainly but I had enough Polish for daily transactions and its acquisition won goodwill at a time when 'events' of '68 affected the writers and theatre people especially. Above all I had the privilege of seeing Grotowski at work, thanks to Peter Brook and Martin Esslin's references. I saw his *Apocalypse Cum Figuris* five times and was able to speak with him twice for hour-long sessions. He preserved his mystique throughout, and the person who was most helpful was the leading actor Riszard Cieslak, whose English is very good. This made the idea of 'workshop' or Grotowski's 'teatr-laboratorium' gell in my mind as an ideal 'learning by discovery' way of running a class. It could be a hold-all of critical and creative development. It offered interactions between *animateur* and group in a more informal mode than that of the traditional class; it could be the way in to understand texts before moving on to casting and rehearsing, it offered time to explore through improvisation the characters, themes and styles, and so much besides

In the autumn of 1969 I persuaded the Department to lay on a six-week course (extended to 12) called Polonnaise: 'a theatre workshop exercise by The Company of the Way' in which information on the history, politics and cultural Polish background led to improvisations. The material ranged from the Captain in Hamlet's, 'We go to gain a little patch of ground that hath no profit in it' etc. to quotes like Wyspianski's, 'These Poles only play Chopin and pray', and included scenes from texts banned in Poland. I hope there are a few people around who understand present-day Poland a bit better for this project. This led to a further series of weekly classes to prepare, rehearse and present *Tango* by Mrozek, a play then banned in Poland since it satirises the anarchy of Polish history and the triumph of red barbarism. This could not be confined only to members of the Company, however, because Department provision must be open to the public. Members of the Company did join, of course, to make a reliable nucleus even if they had now to pay fees. It was 10s. to new students and 5s. for Company members, but this is 20 years ago!. For this they had a ten-week period of general training leading to a production of the Polish parable in the recently built Middleton Hall. I presented the play end-staged and the porters put out all the available rostra to create a projecting apron so that audience and performers shared the same space. It made for tricky long entrances, but the acoustics were far better and the scope for movement and grouping was enhanced. The cast included a newcomer, John Siddle, who proved a great discovery; he was to play leads in many other Theatre Workshop productions. Others in the cast were Margaret Clarke, Christine Johnson, John French, Peter Phillips, Peter Hamilton and Tricia Hern. We paid for Peter and John to have tango lessons since a final scene required them to perform this together! I was particularly glad that other members of the Company of the Way did so much back stage and administrative work for the show. The props were demanding since they represented the 'attic' of Polish history. I recall an elk's head, a Boer War sword, an ancient pram, piles of Polish newspapers and a Polish wedding crown. We covered the screens with montages of Polish newspapers, historical documents and the Polish eagle, the dominant colours being red and white.

The success of this production and the publicity given to the Workshop that preceded it meant that in Autumn, 1970, when the next season's Workshop started its 24 meetings we had an influx of 28 members, many new to the area, young and with as many men as women. We met again in the 'Laboratory', the old wooden hut which was such an asset to us and to the Drama Department for the next five years. It was then knocked down in spite of all our appeals. We were moved to the more luxurious but at first inhibiting surroundings of the new Assembly Hall in Staff House.

By now in 1970-71, what with the opening-up to the public and putting the course on a fee-paying basis, it was needful for to change its name to the more accurate 'Theatre Workshop'. The Company of the Way had a 15-year history of original and distinguished work but the change was inevitable if I was to continue to direct and to be the drama tutor. A few people maybe regretted this but one tried to keep the Company going and I think gradually most recognised that Theatre Workshop was a renewal of the Company's traditions, appreciating the gains we had to offer under the new dispensation. I certainly felt this next phase to be a logical development of what had gone before.

**THEATRE WORKSHOP extramural initiatives in theory and practice**

The Theatre Workshop's classes developed more completely the methods used in directing for The Company of the Way. But drama classes were being provided by the Department all over its large extramural area, since the Head of Department, Professor G. E. T. Mayfield, had first become one of its tutors in 1928. He was head of the Department from 1945 to 1960 and appreciated all aspects of theatre in theory and practice. He especially valued the art of the dramatist, too often neglected even by lovers of theatre as performance. He appointed me in 1946 on the grounds of my theatre experience as well as the required degree in English literature. He even saw to it that I extended this experience as an actress by spring and summer work with the Bristol Old Vic and the studio there, followed by another spell the next year at Windsor Rep, then study with Rudolf Laban in Manchester and Esme Church in Bradford. Later he and Professor W. E. Styler, who followed him in 1960, appointed other full-time drama tutors like Monica Simms (who later became head of B.B.C. Children's TV), and John Styan (Professor of three successive chairs of English in the U.S. and author of many books on drama), Wilhelm Marckwald (a refugee from Nazi Germany who had worked with Reinhardt and in the German cinema), and Brian Clarke (author of *Whose Life Is It Anyway?* and other plays).

We provided weekly classes, residential schools and lecturers on all aspects of drama. The longest running and most successful were our summer ones held at Bretton College of Education and other places between 1948 and 1972. There we could use our own team, augmented by other drama specialists like John Hodgson, who worked with us regularly, and later Mike Walton and Donald Roy joined us when the Hull Drama Department was established. We also had visiting lecturers like Martin Esslin, Clifford Williams, Michael Meyer, Stephen Joseph, Colin Scase, Mike Leigh, Alan Plater and Andrew Cruickshank (just before the *Dr. Finlay* series!). We enrolled students from all over the country with a regular contingent of overseas students. There was always a group from Hull, and the intensive learning that is a special bonus of such a summer school gave them experience that showed in directing and acting for their local societies.

I am putting the Hull Theatre Workshop in this larger context to underline its part in a Departmental regional policy of drama education for adults. The subject tutors for such classes have to provide their own syllabus or scheme of work with a list of texts to be used. My scheme for Theatre Workshop in 1973/4, for example, will do to illustrate one session's programme. Each session was different, however, so I would like to give an account afterwards of the year leading up to a production of *The Cherry Orchard* in 1976.

The 1973 syllabus indicates that we would be 'discovering drama' in two stages. Firstly, the development of group awareness and the extension of imagination and senses without any text: we began, as did every TW course, with relaxation, prone on the floor to overcome tension, mental 'business' and to liberate the body through 'imaging'. This was also a chance to introduce basic teaching on how the voice works. Then came a limbering up period, either in free movement to music, or in finding how changing walks, posture, and using the face as a simple mask, could be germinal to the creation of characters. There followed improvisation work in small groups given general ideas, situations or short phrases: this year produced a memorable series depicting myths, legends and rituals.

The second stage of the class was the study of two or more playtexts. I see that in this 1973/4 sessions we worked on scenes from Pinter's *The Homecoming*, Lope de Vega's *Fuente Ovejuna* and Rudkin's *Afore Night Fall*. Here we used a different kind of improvisation, rooted in the text. This prompted more discussion, taking on matters like thematic structure, the subtext, the style implicit in the dramatist's notation, the nature of the theatre current at a given time, its audiences, the characters whether as individuals or types, the way to build up climaxes, anything that subsumes under the words drama or theatre. By now they were familiar enough with each other and with me to be relaxed and vocal. The polarity that can exist between those who come to act and those whose interests are spread over the whole art of theatre, including reading and going to the theatre, was less noticeable.

By Christmas we were discussing which play we could present when I was approached by the chairman of St. Mary's, Cottingham, parish council. Would we present a play as part of their celebration of the 600th anniversary of the building of the present church?. A few years earlier I had worked on a theatre ballad about the Tolpuddle Martyrs at a summer school, and this idea was put before the Theatre Workshop class. They preferred this challenge to a production of an existing text and someone pointed out that the project could be adapted to our group so that everyone who wanted could take part. This is how the theatre ballad which we called *Six Hundred Years Ago and More* began.

One Sunday therefore we went for a walk around Cottingham and finished up sharing our impressions over beers in the Duke of Cumberland. We decided to focus on the 14th century when Nicholas de Luda was installed as Rector and when he began the building. An epilogue on Cottingham today could be added. In our weekly class we collated what students had found out from such local historians as Ted Gillett and John Whitehouse and treated episodes in experimental improvisations. Those who enjoyed writing polished up some of the best inventions, choruses and songs, and we discovered who could sing, play an instrument and dance and so on to give as varied a 'total theatre' approach as we could. We had in mind the popular audiences, including children, that might see the piece. Beryl Barrett talked to older inhabitants and collected some remarkable memories of the village 50 years before. People made up verses for a ballad to be sung to the tune of *Scarborough Fair* which would link all the episodes together. Gillian Holtby designed costumes which were made by the ladies of the parish. Ian Hey and Sam Lusby, who both lived in Cottingham, kept finding fresh anecdotes and inspired many of the most successful scenes. But it was fun to see how everyone could contribute something. We had a rather phlegmatic French assistant called Claude who could use his native language in the role of the Theobald de Trecis, and who startled us all by the rhodomontade he made up. We reluctantly threw out a riotous pantomine made up just before Christmas based on the story of one Samson, a poor clerk abducted by wicked knights and held in Baynard Castle. It had a chorus of the Beverley Sisters in full habit. However, the research provided some other attractive material and larger themes: a corrupt priory possessed amongst its relics 'the girdle of the Blessed Virgin in a healthy state of pregnancy, an arm of St. George and a piece of the true Cross'. There was also a scene set in Haltemprice Priory where the Abbot hears the confession of one Robert Firthby, a canon fined by the Manor Court for 'attacking John Peynter with club and dagger in Northgate'. The improvised dialogue and business invented by the group was only roughly transcribed to keep its freshness, and the job of prompting was hairier than usual. The play started with the actors entering from the vestry and slowly moving forward onto the acting area as the guitarist played the *Scarborough Fair* tune. The cast stood in a church-shaped group as one read a quotation from the traveller, Leland, who wrote in 1540, 'On great uplands lies the town of Cottingham ... all the ground it is low, very fruitful of meadow and pasture'. Different voices then took up these and other details beginning with the trees, the springs, the woods, the flowers, the meadow lands and the animals. Other scenes showed the building of the church in a mime and dance sequence to an *Estampe Real* which gives it a jolly thumping vigour. We wanted to recall figures in a medieval illuminated manuscript. Someone read up the ritual that accompanied the installation of a rector and we persuaded the then rector to play Nicholas de Luda who was presented to his cure by the Black Prince.

Parody came into the quarrel between Hull and Cottingham, Anlaby and Willerby (CAW) over the water supplies. Here fiction struggles to keep up with farcical historical fact. We did it in the style of *It's a Knock Out*, with Eddie Waring presiding from the pulpit. Buckets of water were carried back and forth in the aisles, fought over, polluted by deadcats and night soil, and the Pope intervened, playing a 'joker' by threatening excommunication. In our version the CAW team won. There were episodes showing the Black Death, the travelling players, the floods, the anarchical rides of the 'black knights' with names like Hugh de Ake, John of Holderness, Hugh Wattefray, Ughtred le Fitz. The action was presented with great flexibility and fluency using the whole church from pulpit to font, aisle to choir, and even the upper reaches overhead.

There were 15 in the cast and a crew of six back stage. Props and costumes were stashed in a big costume basket, dipped into at the beginning, but the organisation back stage had to be good, for we also placed all the extra props and robes in their right places around the church for successive episodes. This access to gear is one of the hazards of free staging. An actor's nightmare is to find say that he or she has a gap filled by spectators between their entry point and some vital cloak, documents or bucket required for that entry.

The play finished with a reading of Philip Larkin's *Churchgoing*. Members of the audience used to come and ask what it was called, who wrote it and could they have a copy. Our theatre ballad was greatly enjoyed too. The TW team could look back on their months on hard work with a real sense of achievement, and some of us agreed that the preparation brought as much pleasure as the performances.

Our other productions were big scale classics, with the exception of two six-week summer courses on *Othello* and *Lear*. This was when circumstances made it difficult for me to commit myself to a full-scale production. These Shakespeare projects were not for public showing, but a method of understanding the text and its subtext through practical work. We took Acts One and Two of *Lear*, selecting focal speeches and images. From these we created a montage on a giant chess board, revealing characters, relationships, the power struggle through a pattern of verbal and non-verbal means,

Our other productions originated in class study of stage classics or controversial contemporary work. Amongst these were:
1971 *The Plough and the Stars* by Sean O'Casey
1972 *Rites* by Maureen Duffy
    *Sharpeville Sequence* by Edward Bond
1973 *Heartbreak House* by Bernard Shaw
1976 *The Cherry Orchard* by Chekhov

The other aspect of Theatre Workshop's contribution to drama in the community can be illustrated by a look at our 1975/6 class in which we studied and produced Chekhov's *Cherry Orchard*. On the first night of the class we enrolled 10 men and 11 women whose occupations show in our records as housewives, teachers, an accountant, a solicitor, three engineers and one unemployed man. Others joined later. In the first six weeks we worked without any scripts, although, having taken stock of the group, I was excited by the idea of their doing the Chekhov. As always, we started with the relaxation and movement.

I then introduced themes and situations from *The Cherry Orchard* for improvisation in small groups: seasonal change, social hierarchies, status, family and neighbour relationships. By the seventh class we started using the text, which I had asked them to read at home. This is a difficult moment engendered by 'free play' preliminaries, and the group sense that has evolved can be lost when books are in hand: reading is once more 'print-heavy'. Somehow all that imagination and creativity must be kept alive and harnessed to understanding and enjoying what lies behind the printed page. Students knew that this play was a Great Work but the home reading was hard going. Many expressed disappointment, complained about the boring long miserable speeches, the weirdness of these Russians, and the radicals were of the view that the revolutions didn't come soon enough!. There were a few absentees the following week. It's not the best moment for the tutor either. The immediate goal is to get the students to discover an emotional subtext, the action behind the print, and to help them see the scenes described in stage directions. They can come to recognise that these fictions with the odd names may be Russians and from long ago, but their situation, their anxieties, their absurdities, hopes, joys, sorrows and their sense of being trapped in history are analogous with ours. Playing in the round as we did reduced the technical problems of being 'up there' and ensured that the cast could concentrate on their subtext. Being aware of what lies beneath words and silences marks off creative acting from performance. The set was minimal, a bale of straw, simple white furniture, the life in props and effects. Directing 'in the round' is equally liberating, for all its problems.

In Theatre Workshop we had got a long way towards depth playing but beyond that lay the challenge of performing and sharing our experience in public. The responsibility for shaping up to this end had to be mine as tutor/director and at the risk of losing many creative moments found in our earlier relaxed exploring of the text. But this is where I could remind myself of the proposed aims of TW: to work as a group, to understand a major playwright's notation, to help students value the art of theatre to combine the scholarly with the practical, to widen horizons. The resistance to Chekhov (or Shaw or O'Casey or Pinter) was overcome and in its place we were able to see a text as a score to be realised on stage. In this year's study we had been through a 'discovery learning' process. We had also come to appreciate the interpretive arts of actor, director and all the stage cooperative. The final performances were a necessary extension of this process and even 'being directed' was part of it. It wasn't only what the small audiences saw and heard that counted, but the group sense of loving and understanding the play, plus their modest surprise at having reached the standard they did. For the performances had a depth and sensitivity that impressed many who saw them.

Theatre Workshop is one example of the contributions made by both the Department of Adult Education to drama in Hull since 1945 both for amateur practitioners and playgoers. The work done falls into two main categories, although it would be true to say these divisions were never exclusive of each other. It was more a matter of emphasis. In the early years there was academic mistrust of practical work, and the tutors were all appointed in 'literature and drama' so that some classes we took might include a Shakespeare play along with, say, a Jane Austen novel and selected poems. In this context one aimed to increase appreciation of the play as only complete if performed, and the students were often taken to London or Stratford to see it. In the palmy Sixties it was possible to go to both a matinee and an evening performance at the RSC at Stratford and stop over in a rather grotty but jolly ex-army camp at Snitterfield. Or we travelled to Nottingham, Leeds, Sheffield and York to see Brecht, Pirandello, Chekhov Shakespeare, and many others. The local theatres were also supported, but until recently the choice there was limited.

A second category of the work is represented by the day schools, weekends and longer residential schools offering lectures framing a schedule that included movement, mask making, television and seminars on selected plays or themes where the approach was mainly practical. We could not offer a programme of lighting, effects, make-up or set-making only, though occasionally these were asked for. These courses interpreted specific plays, concepts, genres, (Restoration, The Greeks, the Absurd for example) for their staging. In the later Seventies and Eighties, I worked with Robert Protherough of the Institute of Education on linked weekends at Horncastle where many Hull teachers and other amateurs joined like spirits from all over Humberside for intensive practical work with lectures introducing the work of Beckett, Brecht, Shakespeare, Shaw, Ayckbourn and Ibsen. Again this was carrying on the tradition in the Department of encouraging appreciation of drama in the University extramural area. It had depended upon a number of factors, the most important of which was the concern shown by the Head of Department, seen particularly in the full-time appointments made. Literature and drama no longer enjoyed the central position they had under Professors Mayfield and Styler. Now there was a shift to other areas like certificates and degrees in adult education, trade union studies and industrial archaeology. In 1980 there remained two full-time literature specialists and one drama (and literature) tutor, myself. At the time of writing there remained one literature tutor assisted by many fine part-timers. Whilst individually most of these can be first-rate teachers and scholars (no one survives in adult education unless they can keep their students' enthusiasm) and the expense that full-time staff entails has been cut, there are disadvantages. In the past we had a team with the practical expertise needed to teach drama full-time in combination with academic knowledge of the British, American and European theatre past and present plus special knowledge of the needs of adult learners, availability to travel over the large area for which the University of Hull is responsible, a coherent planned programme of classes, weekends and other commitments administered by the team, attendance at conferences, visits to performances of plays, and a wide range of professional theatre contacts: and that team gained strength from its close association in a communal purpose. Drama as a subject was valued and focal to our entire regional programme. Part-time tutors operate in a more random and uncoordinated way by virtue of their other commitments in time and place. In the immediate future even our remaining literature tutor, like his colleagues in philosophy and film, will be moved to internal lectureships in the process of 1990's stringent reduction of the University's School of Adult Education in its present form.

It is with a whimper rather than a bang therefore that this account must end. Yet in reviewing and recording the past one realises how much was achieved and that appraisal may spur others to renew the University's concern for extramural drama education in the future. Providing theatre and all the arts are valued as joyful in themselves, and a means of affirming our individual, social and spiritual growth. Which is what this whole history of community drama in Hull is about.

# CHAPTER TWO

# HULL UNIVERSITY DRAMA DEPARTMENT 1963-1992

by J. Michael Walton

In February, 1966, the *Hull Daily Mail* accepted an invitation to review the first full-length production to be presented by Hull University Drama Department in the recently opened Theatre Laboratory. The rehearsal period of *Under Milk Wood* by Dylan Thomas had not been entirely smooth. The Theatre Laboratory, where the performance was to take place, was the first building the Department could call its own, but was little more than a Nissen hut which had previously served as the University gymnasium. Under-heated and under-equipped, it lacked even toilet facilities, a major consideration when the week of performance coincided with an outbreak of gastric flu' which spread remorselessly through the cast of nearly 50.

The *Mail* review was more than charitable and the following day I phoned to thank the reviewer and ask if she would like to be kept informed about our future work. 'I'm glad to talk to you,' she said. 'There were some things I disliked about the production but we weren't sure, whether you could count as amateur or professional. You see we're not allowed to criticise professionals.' This unexpected dimension to criticism in the provinces took me aback. I had moved to Hull six months before and was still trying falteringly to adjust from the tempo of professional theatre to the more sedate rhythm of a university, and a university at that in a city with no repertory theatre closer than York. Puzzlement about what Drama meant in a university context was something with which I was to become familiar over the next few years.

The following account is, confessedly, a personal view and sometimes, no doubt, a romantic one. It does reflect an enthusiasm for, and a pride in, an academic experiment which has brought credit to a university and to a city, neither of which in the 1960s could by the wildest stretches of the imagination have been regarded nationally as a cradle of the performing arts.

An association between the community of Hull and Hull University in the teaching of drama had been forged within the Department of Adult

Education before the introduction of undergraduate courses, links which other contributors to this book will detail. Britain's experience of university drama, though, was far different from that of the U.S.A., where it had been possible to major in Drama or Theatre from as early as 1920. As far as the British universities were concerned, drama was extramural or recreational. Then Bristol University introduced Drama as a full academic discipline with the appointment of Glynne Wickham in 1948. In the early Sixties Manchester created a Chair of Drama, and in 1963, largely as a result of initiatives from Professors Ray Brett and Garnett Rees, and a sympathetic Vice-Chancellor, Brynmor Jones, Hull became the third University Drama Department with the appointment of Donald Roy who had previously lectured in French at the Universities of Glasgow and St. Andrews. He is currently the first Professor and Director of Drama.

The pioneering work in Hull was conducted largely on a day-to-day basis. As the one member of staff and with a single room in what is now the Administration block, Donald had to build from scratch. The University was not large. Few of the buildings were permanent and the pedigree of awarding University of Hull, as opposed to University of London, degrees stretched back only to 1954. Students enrolling for a Single Honours (Special) degree were required to take at least one Ancillary course lasting for three terms, or a Subsidiary for five. A single member of staff could hope to offer no more than an Ancillary course and in October, 1963, 19 pioneers enrolled for Ancillary Drama.

The basis of the course was theatre history and dramatic literature but Donald believed, as have his colleagues since, that a Drama Department exists in its own right in order to promote the whole process of theatre. Academic study must be tried against practical demonstration and performance. Without such a blend the study could only remain theoretical with a whole dimension ignored. Inevitably this implied the production of plays before a live audience. Drama is, any way, a communal art. The proponents of an independent Drama Department had long argued that Drama was a natural focus, alongside Music, for linking the growing University to a city which had always been wary of it.

The campus had, needless to say, no theatre. Nor did it have anything resembling a theatre space except for what was known as the Assembly Hall, upstairs in the second of the two buildings facing onto Cottingham Road. The other building was where lectures took place, a physical split which was to have a profound effect on the physical dimensions of the first generation of drama students. Male and female alike acquired muscles fit for shot-putters by having to haul solid wooden rostra out of the lecture rooms to the Assembly Hall, and later to the Theatre Laboratory, in order to build an auditorium or provide stage levels. These rostra had been built to last, not for mobility, and they were indispensable for classrooms. Not only did they have to be humped over to where a performance was to take place between the end of the last lecture of the day and curtain-up, but the epilogue, almost the epitaph, to every performance was the dismantling of set and auditorium and hauling all the bits back for the next morning's 9.15 a.m. lectures.

In the spring term of 1964 a triple-bill was mounted in the Assembly Hall consisting of Ian Hamilton's *Walking Through Seaweed*, Edward Albee's *The Sandbox* and T. S. Eliots's *Sweeney Agonistes*. *The Guardian*, in the person of Benedict Nightingale, had none of the *Hull Mail's* problems with the status of the productions but praised them anyway. With a successful first night and the presence of the national press, the Drama Department was truly on its way.

Soon after, a second member of staff was appointed. Harry Thompson, better known recently for his award-winning Radio Four series, *Carry On Up The Fifties*, had a background in front-of-house management at the Mermaid Theatre and lecturing in Fine Art in Nottingham. The one-year Ancillary course was augmented by the five-term Subsidiary and the process of negotiation began for a theatre, however modest, to serve as a base and as a home. My own appointment as third member of staff in 1965 was to complement the specialist interests of those already in post, academically and practically. I came with a degree in Classics, but from working as an actor and director in the professional theatre.

In the first two years great strides forward had been made. The University was growing fast and a grand new Sports Centre opened on Inglemire Lane. The former gymnasium, which we now inherited as our theatre, was little more than a prefab with a corrugated iron roof. A hailstone was capable of bringing a performance to a dead halt. The walls were only part brick, but solid enough to support the wall bars which we asked to have left in place as an anchor-point for scenery and lighting. The other reason for leaving them was not wholly groundless fear that, were the bars removed, the whole building might collapse. We re-christened the old Gymnasium, the Theatre Laboratory.

In September, 1965, before term began and before the Old Gymnasium looked much like a Theatre Laboratory, a letter arrived inviting the Department to host a production of Brecht's *The Threepenny Opera* by the Janacek Academy of Brno in Chechoslovakia. Getting the building ready to house any production, never mind a prestige production from Eastern Europe backed by the British Council and the British Drama League, seemed barely feasible when term began. Harry Thompson's memo's to the Building Office became pithier as December 1st drew near:

'Dear Mr Blanchard,

I don't know whether anyone has nipped into the Theatre Lab and hung the shower curtains since I was in there yesterday — if not, I would ask if they might be in position by Wednesday midday. Otherwise we look like having a more widely applauded show in the showers than on the stage.'

The arrival of the Brno company with an enormous set but no interpreter was another occasion for the exercise of tact, as Harry took away the intransigent director to show him anything but the theatre, while the Czech stage-manager and I found a compromise between having no audience and having no play. Restricted or not, the production turned out to be a splendid one and showed, somewhat to the surprise of us all, that the Theatre Laboratory was a wonderful theatre space. Tatty and makeshift it might look from the outside — the University subsequently pulled it down as an eyesore which would look prettier as a car park — it was precisely what the Department needed at the time.

The repertoire of the Theatre Lab was impressive, with two productions or bills in most terms as the numbers studying Drama grew and those who had completed their short courses with us continued to lend their support.

The concept of a production being an aspect of research was one that the University in general took many years to entertain, an attitude which led to much of our work being welcomed as an exotic sideshow but nothing more. Drama Department staff were under no doubt that experiments into questions of stage space and actor/audience relationships were of a high seriousness. But the subject was still regarded in some quarters as a hybrid which infringed on more traditional disciplines without requiring their rigour: and students would keep blaming late rehearsals for the failure to submit essays on time. The tightrope between art and academe was a delicate one to walk, particularly when the right to fail was enshrined in the right to experiment.

The flexibility of the building was tested to its limit with another British première, him by the American poet e.e. cummings (one of whose eccentricities was never to use capital letters). This weird, pre-absurdist, post-expressionist farce is set in the mind of one of the characters during the birth of her first child. Staged in a circus ring with film sequences and a quarter of a mile of mirror plastic, the elaborate preparation nearly foundered with less than a week to the opening night. The play had been written in 1926 and, though permission for the British rights had been sought over six months before, no reply had been forthcoming. A final letter stating that, unless we heard otherwise, we would assume that we could do the play provoked a letter from cummings' widow demanding royalties that exceeded the entire show's budget. A panic-stricken phone call to the American Embassy met a generous and instantaneous response offering to pay the royalties. We had our first 'sponsored' production.

In a time when so many arts organisations are starved for cash it is sometimes salutary to remember how little experimental theatre took place anywhere in Britain in the early 1960s, and how comparatively unfamiliar ideas of subsidy seemed. The explosion of pub theatres, studio theatres and small-scale touring was still on a long fuse. The Edinburgh Festival with a Fringe a fifth of its current size was a rare feast. Productions from the early

Drama Departments attracted national attention by extending the repertoire, particularly to work from Europe and America. Their graduates have played a major role in expanding that repertoire still further. Hull's lack of a permanent theatre company in the mid- to late-Sixties was to our advantage, but I like to think that the spirit of experiment that we engendered, as well as the students we produced, provided one of the platforms which made Hull Truck and Remould possible.

The treatment of our work as both research and experiment made us aware of a paradox that existed in our attitude to our audiences. From the first production and until well into the Seventies we always offered free admission. We held the belief, rightly or wrongly, that the nature of our work could be compromised if box-office returns became a factor in either the choice of play or the method in which it was to be presented. Such idealism could hardly have survived into the hard world of the Eighties, but it does highlight a problem we have always encountered in the presentation of productions within the degree structure. If students are preparing and presenting performances, either as an additional element to their course work or as an accessible part of that work, then the imperative posed by a paying audience must be a feature of those performances. Demanding money for a ticket implies a contract to supply a certain amount of entertainment. As a discipline in learning the processes of production, that is fine in its way. In terms of the exploration of a dramatic idea or text, it may handicap experiment and undoubtedly does contribute to the risk of a star system in casting.

Now in 1991, there is no question of not charging for any public production. Budgets are geared to box-office returns and productions are expected, hidden costs apart, to pay for themselves. A play with moderate audience appeal may have to be re-programmed and budgeted alongside a more commercial proposition. This affects both staff and student directed plays. That we take it for granted is a mark of the times.

There is, however, one area where we maintained the principles of a bygone era and feel we need not be bound or influenced by the finished quality of the product. That area is the Huddle, the Department's name for a lunching performance with restricted resources and, outside Hull, the best known of all our activities.

A lack of professional contact was one of the shortcomings of the Department in its formative years. Opportunities to visit professional productions were few or involved considerable travelling. More importantly for students studying Drama as part or whole of their degree programme, there were few occasions when they could meet and talk with those engaged with the profession to which the majority aspired. To combat this it became the custom to invite up to the University professional actors, directors, writers or administrators who found themselves working in the area. Lunchtime was also the obvious time for the showing of small-scale

22

experimental work. The atmosphere and informality resulted in such occasions being known as 'huddles'. It was only when the name had become established as part of our jargon that Donald Roy, on being challenged by a member of staff from another department about the place of something called a 'huddle' in academic life, replied, off the top of his head, that 'huddle' was an acronym for Hull University Drama Department Lunchtime Event. So huddles became Huddles and part of the folklore.

Once the Department productions programme was fully established and the number of students had increased to the point where full productions of all work could not be accommodated, the Huddle tended more towards the performance of student work for a strictly in-house audience. The more social function had never disappeared entirely, I am happy to say, and we owe an enormous debt of gratitude to all those who have submitted to having their brains and memories picked and, just occasionally, to facing more mischievous student questions. All we have been able to offer in return is a quick bite of lunch and a cup of coffee. Those professionals who live locally have offered unstinting support to the Department and I have never known Alan Plater, Mike Bradwell, Barrie Nettleton, John Godber or Rupert Creed turn down an invitation to talk to students, unless irrevocably committed elsewhere.

From visiting actors and actresses there have been some spectacular Huddles with indiscretions and revelations flying about like confetti. Hollywood star of the Forties, Veronica Lake, arrived with an acolyte whose only task was to keep the great lady's glass filled. Sir Donald Wolfit, whose mood we had been warned to humour, was all meekness and charm until a naive first-year asked him why he had never appeared with the National Theatre. As Wolfit had believed for years before there was an National Theatre that he was the National Theatre incarnate, the afternoon soured. Michael macLiammoir claimed he wanted to run off with our Stage Manager, David Edwards. Harry H. Corbett arrived grumpier than the hard-pressed Harold Steptoe had ever been. Slumped in a chair, glowering, he threatened to provoke the longest silence in theatre history, until an inspired voice from the back asked where he had bought his suit, a sort of George Melly cast-off that would have made a bookie's runner wince. The briefest of pauses, then Corbett burst out laughing and proceeded to talk for a fascinating hour on what life was like in Joan Littlewood's Theatre Workshop.

Ian Carmichael and the late Sir Anthony Quayle, both honorary graduates of the University, Donald Sinden, Patricia Routledge, Susan Hampshire, Nat Jackley, Michael Denison and Dulcie Gray, as well as various members of the RSC and the National Theatre Company proved fascinating and informative guests who have genuinely seemed to welcome the chance to speak off the record.

With the transformation of the Old Gymnasium into the Theatre

Laboratory the Department had its first home and a sense of identity. Academics and students, with little concept of the work we might do, found a product available to them in public productions which was more consistent and more adventurous than anything to be found in a student dramatic society. Fostering a regular audience from outside took more time but our mailing list eventually contained 600 names. It is a source of considerable pleasure that some of our current audiences have memories of Drama Department productions stretching back 25 or more years and think of them as nostalgically as the staff who worked on them. From more recent times several can remember Sarah Greene's first performance, Tim Reed's first set design, Bob Carlton's first performance or Anthony Minghella's first play, *Mobius the Stripper*, when the Theatre Lab looked at its best, transformed into a seedy nightclub. As significant for the theatre in Hull was the constant stream of actors and technicians who became members of Hull Truck. The company has seldom been without at least one Hull Drama graduate, and the Gulbenkian Theatre hosted several of the early productions.

Other graduates created companies of their own to fill the gap in educational and community drama in Humberside. Rupert Creed gained a first-class degree in Drama and German before deciding to co-form Remould, a company whose success has been as notable, if not yet international, as that of Hull Truck. Commitments within the University confined regular ventures by the Department into the Community to occasional tours but the enthusiasm with which new students took to Hull, 'outsiders' from all over Britain, from Europe, Asia, Africa, Australasia, North and South America, has surely contributed to the City's enhanced image of recent years.

Two new members of staff in 1966, David Edwards and John Harris, made it possible to begin teaching Drama as part of a joint Honours course lasting for three years. A majority of students were shared with the Department of English but combinations were available with American Studies, Greek or Latin, Music, Theology and a range of modern languages. By 1965 the Ancillary class had topped the 50 mark. Twenty-three enrolled for the first Joint degree course in 1966. In 1967, by a selection aberration, we had our first-year intake of 39, three-quarters of whom were women, from some 800 applicants. The course was at that time still chronologically based, a survey of theatre history and dramatic literature from Classical Greece to the present day. Selection of plays for performance was geared more to the specific interests of individual staff and the kind of challenges posed by the theatre itself.

On the campus the need had long been felt for a more suitable venue for concerts and public lectures. Peter Brook had had to deliver the talks that were subsequently published as *The Empty Space* in the Assembly Hall, less an empty space than a void. As a result, the Middleton Hall was designed as a multi-purpose university theatre to be situated alongside the newly-constructed Arts Block. The auditorium of the Middleton Hall holds over 400, and the stage, if inflexible for drama purposes, does have room for an organ. Downstairs is a circulation area, the University chapel and a home for the University's impressive Art Collection. As a compromise between the varying demands made upon it, the Middleton Hall has proved to have many merits. The Drama Department tends to leave it to the others but the biennial opera is staged there in association with the major users of the auditorium, the Department of Music. Sir Brynmor Jones, under whose aegis as Vice-Chancellor the Department had been inaugurated, and whose wife later donated the Dora Jones Prize for the outstanding practical student of the year, felt that a drama production would be appropriate for the formal opening of the Middleton Hall, but one that was not exclusively from the Drama Department.

Accordingly, Hull Theatre Group was formed with the enthusiastic support of Donald Campbell, the Buildings Officer, and Frank Harris-Jones, Deputy Registrar and a prominent local amateur actor. The Drama Department was joined in the enterprise by the Students' Union Dramatic Society and also by the Company of the Way, in order to create a true town-and-gown feel. Invited to direct the inaugural production, I chose Chekov's *The Seagull*. A gala opening on June 15th 1967 before an impressive assembly of civic dignitaries was boosted by a personal guarantee which proved unnecessary, and Hull Theatre Group was to present two further productions in subsequent years, Ionesco's *Exit the King* and Giraudoux's *The Enchanted*, directed respectively by Frank Harris-Jones and Gill Holtby.

By 1969 the Department was engaged in further expansion. This was the year which saw our first set of graduates, and the Midsummer Festival at which Hull Theatre Group gave their final production also featured a company called Theatre Laboratory 66. This consisted of the majority of that first bunch of guinea-pigs, clasping their unique pieces of paper and heading for the big time: or so they hoped. We acquired the rights to the first British Production of *The Sunday Walk* by Georges Michel, in a translation by Jean Benedetti, and toured to the York Festival, then down to London for two weeks at the minute Little Theatre, Garrick Yard, off St. Martin's Lane and up about two hundred stairs. Small venues were rare then but Harold Hobson, as brave as ever, tackled the ascent and descent to demonstrate in *The Sunday Times* his abiding enthusiasm for modern French theatre.

So the first phase of the Department's growth was complete but we had no time to stand still. The new generation of students coming up the following autumn were to find something much grander than the Theatre Lab as their base as we moved into a new purpose-built complex, the Gulbenkian Centre, which remains the Department's home.

In the pre-planning stage Donald Roy and Donald Campbell had visited several drama studios, at Bristol, LAMDA and Goldsmith's College, but none of these seemed particularly exciting as a theatre space. The early Sixties was a barren period for experimental staging and it was difficult to as much as find an architect with any experience of designing a theatre. Eventually they approached Peter Moro, architect of the Nottingham Playhouse which had opened in 1964. Moro accepted the commission with enthusiasm, though there must be some doubt if he would have been quite so keen had he foreseen the subsequent problems.

The money required to build a Drama Studio and the money available from the University Grants Committee (U.G.C.) to pay for it were miles apart. Nor was the Committee altogether convinced that the University needed another theatre so soon after the opening of the Middleton Hall. They did agree to equip a Studio Theatre if capital funding could be found from elsewhere. Donald Roy described what happened next in the booklet, *Hull University Drama Department, 21st Birthday, 1984:* 'At this stage the then Vice-Chancellor, Sir Brynmor Jones, made the shrewd lateral-thinking suggestion that the drama studio, which naturally contained facilities for radio and television, might be combined with the University's projected audio-visual centre. Back to the drawing board fore several months. But they were months well spent because it was with this revised plan that Sir Brynmor eventually managed to interest the Gulbenkian Foundation, who were impressed by the originality of the dual-purpose concept and decided to make us a grant of £50,000 towards its realisation.'

The spur of such an offer against a deadline for the start of the work led to a flurry of planning and tendering. The designs had to be shrunk by 18 inches all round, which sounds little, but resulted in the loss of a proper rehearsal room. Most of the original features, strenuously challenged by the U.G.C., survived, and in the end the only victims were the comfort of the audience and uncommitted space for expansion. We hung on grimly to the fly tower, the full counter-weight flying system, the gallery with its paintbridge, the stage basement and orchestra pit. These were all in the Studio Theatre constructed back to back with a television studio and control rooms. In the north-west of the building, adjacent to the television studio was a small radio studio. Workshop space was shared between the Drama Department and the Audio-Visual Centre and there was room for individual staff-rooms as well as a wardrobe, dressing room and a foyer.

The completion of the Gulbenkian Centre in the summer of 1969 put an end to such anxieties. Suddenly the University possessed a complex which the Gulbenkian Foundation were prepared to boast had no rival in Europe as a teaching theatre. Architects and academics arrived from as far away as Australia and Canada to see what tips they could glean for their own proposed Studio Theatres. The technical aspects of the theatre, devised by Richard Pilbrow and Theatre Projects, were much admired, particularly the flexible proscenium towers and the speed with which a variety of stage and auditorium shapes could be rigged. The whole building remains a tribute to Peter Moro's inspiration as well as to his stamina.

The exhausting summer tour with Theatre Laboratory 66 was followed by hectic preparations for a new session with a vacation course production whose venue was still uncertain. Viv Bridson, who was to join the department as a dance specialist, John Harris and I worked on two Greek plays, Aeschylus' *Libation-Bearers* and Euripides' *Electra*, presented in contrasting styles. The Aeschylus had a full chorus, masks and heightened speech patterns. The Euripides was as realistic as it was possible to get within the dictates of the original text. It was less than a week before we opened that we received confirmation that the productions could be played in the new Studio Theatre.

The first audience entered the building with a sense of wonder, especially those who had followed us in the Theatre Lab. The stage looked so vast. The first play used an open acting area confined only by a cyclorama and the proscenium towers opened to form a flat skene with three doors. After the interval the audience returned to a conventional proscenium arch and front tabs with a naturalistic setting. The genuine versatility of the building had proved itself within a week.

The official opening, six months later, when all the paint was dry, further tested that versatility with the re-creation of the entire bill as performed at the Theatre Royal, Hull in 1820, 150 years before. Planche's *The Vampire* or *The Bride of the Isles* used traps and flown characters. Mrs Inchbald's comedy *The Wedding Day* followed and the evening concluded with the Thomas Didbin farce *Of Age Tomorrow*. A splendid evening in the presence of civic and university dignitaries was enhanced by the visit of colleagues from other Drama Departments who came to admire and congratulate us on our new premises and left unashamedly envious.

The strides which Drama had made as an academic subject by this time, in Hull and in other universities, were soon confirmed by our following Manchester into the teaching of a full Single Honours or Special degree. The Gulbenkian was never granted the necessary technical staff to run it to its potential, but with a full academic staff of six and a Centre Services Unit of four shared with the Audio-Visual Centre, it was possible to broaden the technical aspects of the courses and help all students acquire some knowledge of how to handle the building. Inevitably this gave a more vocational slant to the degree course, the only disappointment being amongst those students who left expecting to find facilities as good elsewhere. For an all too brief time we had the Theatre Lab as well as the Gulbenkian, and Anthony Minghella, a student from 1972 and later a member of staff, was able to pick up the challenge of writing for each as a different theatre space with *Mobius the Stripper* and *Whale Music*.

The next few years were years of consolidation. The concentration we had put into creating a unique working environment had been, to a great extent, at the expense of traditional published research. Professor Glynne Wickham, founder of the first British Drama Department at Bristol University, warned us of the need to tackle publication in earnest if only to provide a protection should the time come when university expansion could no longer be taken for granted. But writing books and articles takes time and there was never a year in which revision of courses and the developments of new initiatives in teaching did not take up a major part of every vacation, including summer vacations already curtailed by vacation courses at either end. However we might argue that the presentation of a play in performance was as proper a piece of research as an article in a learned journal, it was only grudgingly that direction or design were allowed as 'an element in but not a substitute for published research'. Even then the principle seemed hardly observed in practice and it was not until 26 years after the funding of the Department, and the third Vice-Chancellor after Sir Brynmor Jones, that the Department was awarded a developmental Chair.

Whatever the other concerns of the Department in terms of teaching or providing a cultural service within the community, the Gulbenkian has remained a place for legitimate theatre research. In 1973 a Restoration theatre was recreated on the stage floor for *From Pit Bench to Gallery*. Numerous new translations have been performed in the Studio Theatre, only to become 'acceptable' as academic work when enshrined in print. The fact that a production might enthral, terrorise or amuse 1,000 people in a week was for far too long regarded as nothing compared to the value of an article in a journal which might be read by six scholars in six months.

The sense that the work we were doing was somehow improper in a university was compounded by a similar suspicion on the part of the professional theatre that we were intellectuals or dilettantes rather than practitioners. Perhaps we contributed to the confusion by being the only Drama Department in which all academic staff taught some aspect of practical theatre, and where technical and even secretarial staff have been involved in the teaching programme. Productions may have varied in quality over the years, but there has always been an attempt to extend the teaching process by treating productions as research into stage space, theatrical effect or period style, where the response of an audience should be the test of the work. Much of it rubbed off when our students graduated, many of them into theatre-in-education or community theatre work where they could develop their own ideas from the basic grammar of theatre we explored with them.

The price we paid, or nearly paid, for according so little attention to the advice of Professor Wickham was to be taken by surprise when the first university cuts were announced in 1981. Seven of the universities where Drama was taught to degree level had been recommended to close down their courses. Hull was one of the seven.

The ensuing hullabaloo is more exciting in retrospect than it was at the time. The University and most of the staff rallied to our support. Alan Ayckbourn fortuitously was receiving an honorary degree at the July degree ceremony and publicly called for the recommendation to be rejected. The Gulbenkian Foundation, whose United Kingdom Director happened to be one of our graduates, gave a forceful reaction to the prospect of the Centre being used for purposes other than those for which they had donated money. The Vice-Chancellor, Sir Roy Marshall, used this as a platform for a broad campaign of support. The outcome was both happy and sad. Drama was saved in Hull, as it was elsewhere, but the next round of UGC 'advice' was more prescriptive and has led to the demise in Hull of a number of strong and valuable disciplines, many of whose members, now retired or relocated, were among the most vociferous in defence of Drama.

At the time of writing, the future of the Department appears secure, but the lack of forward funding and planning for Higher Education makes everyone wary of the whims of the latest education minister. Drama as an academic discipline would appear to be more likely to fall victim to its popularity than to government disapproval. Wave upon wave of applicants has guaranteed us students of the highest calibre, many choosing Hull in preference to Oxbridge or the better professional schools. Higher and higher staff/student ratios and diminished technical help threaten to submerge all the principles of individual teaching and opportunity on which the Department was established.

Since 1981 we have learned to be chameleons, as strolling players always had to be, prepared to adapt to whatever new philosophy current thinking was dreaming up. Our research rating has risen with the publication of books and articles. We offer a semi-vocational M.A. course and currently welcome an annual B.Ed. intake of second-year students from the Bishop Grosseteste College in Lincoln. All of this puts extra strain on a building which was never meant to cope with the requirements of upwards of 150 students in any one year. Donald Roy, John Harris and I have been here since the days of the Theatre Laboratory, joined later by Tony Meech, Robert Cheesmond and Keith Peacock, making up a complement of six academic staff. Two of the four Centre Services posts have been axed, but the long-term support of Jim Lambert has kept the theatre safe, operative and imaginatively used, while Ruth Stuckley in the Wardrobe, and Barbara Carmichael and Noreen Frankland in the Departmental Office have successfully run a theatre alongside a teaching department.

If the future is unknowable rather than uncertain, then we can at least look to a past of achievement in terms of our own work and that of our graduates.

The Department has toured abroad and widely throughout Britain. Hardly an Edinburgh Festival of National Student Drama Festival has gone by in the last 20 years without Department students making a prominent contribution and picking up awards, often under the touring name of 'Z' Theatre Company.

Our students have become members of the National Theatre Company, the Royal Shakespeare Company, the Royal Court, Glasgow Citizens and every major professional company in the country. Eight former students are making a living out of writing for the stage, film and television. Twenty-one were featured on radio or television over the Christmas period of 1990. There was one occasion when, simultaneously, the directors of *Brookside*, *Eastenders* and *Coronation Street* were all graduates of our Department. Former students have picked up awards from *Plays and Players* and *The Evening Standard*, and won an Emmy, a Bafta, an Italian Prize, a Sony and an Olivier.

There is a host too of students who will never see their names in lights and who may never have looked for a career that would bring them public acclaim. The Department and the work we promote offers a chance for them to study for three years a subject dear to them but in a place where any lack of creative and performing talent does not automatically disqualify them from the value of the study.

Hull was once a city renowned for its theatres. By the 20th century such enthusiasm has diminished, kept alive largely, though by no means exclusively, by pockets of resistance amongst those for whom theatre was not a living but a hobby. Powerful as the amateur movement may still be, there is a need for a community to have a professional input if the rest of the country is to take its theatre seriously.

Thanks to the success of Hull Truck and Remould, Hull's professional theatre is firmly on the map. I should like to think that the work of the Drama Department since 1963 has helped to put it there. We have sent generations of graduates from all over the country, indeed all over the world, into places where theatre work has traditionally flourished. They have carried with them an affection for the area and a sense of having belonged here, however briefly. More importantly, I believe that we established a climate through the Drama Department in which it was possible for companies like Hull Truck and Remould to see Hull as a home base, rather than an accommodation address. When the Department opened, national critics came to review our shows, attracted by the novelty that anything should be taking place in such an outpost. Now they come regularly to Spring Street knowing that work first seen in Hull could become the toast of Los Angeles. Students elect to come to Hull's two universities, students of any subject, because, amongst other things, Hull is a place where live theatre is seen to flourish. May we long continue in the Drama Department to provide a continuity, a tradition and an inspiration within the University and within the City.

Noah *at St. Mary's Church, Lowgate, Hull, 1956. The Company of the Way's first production.*

*Costume designs by Nancy Lamplugh for the Company of the Way's production of* Candle in the Heavens, *1958.*

*The chorus of 'Women of Whitby', during a performance at the Retreat House at Ryedale of* Candle in the Heavens. *The Celtic cross was designed and made of papier maché by Oliver Webb.*

31

*The Company of the Way in the* The Birthday Party, *1962. Meg (Suzanne Robinson), Stanley (David Welch), Petey (Bertram Woods). The first non-professional production.*
(*Photograph by courtesy of the* Hull Daily Mail)

*Alan Plater discusses his anthology,* Made in Hull, *with Colin Edwynn and Elizabeth Ashton at Keldgate Arts Centre, Beverley, 1966. The background exhibition is by Simon Goldberg.*
(*Photograph by courtesy of the* Hull Daily Mail)

*The Company of the Way in* The Alchemist, *with Doll Common played by Pamela Dellar, Face by Frank Harris-Jones and Subtle by Peter Redford, 1964.*
(*Photograph by courtesy of the* Hull Daily Mail)

*Above: Brenda Walker as Dame Pliant in* The Alchemist.

*Top: Muriel Crane giving notes to the cast of* The Alchemist *in the University Assembly Hall.*
*(Photograph by courtesy of the* Hull Daily Mail*)*

*Left: Dorothy Wilson and Ray Williams in the Adult Education Department Theatre Workshop production of* The Cherry Orchard.

Sir Anthony Quayle with Professor Donald Roy and Dr. J. Michael Walton.

(*Photograph by courtesy of the Brynmor Jones Library*)

*Hull Theatre Group in* The Seagull *, The Middleton hall, 1967, and The Theatre Laboratory.*

*Sarah Greene as Polly Peachum in the Drama Department's production of Brecht's* Threepenny Opera, 1977. *(Photograph by courtesy of A. J. Mecch)*

*The Department on Tour.* A Trip to Scarborough *by R. B. Sheridan, at Beningbrough Hall, 1986.*

*(Photograph by courtesy of the Brynmor Jones Library)*

# CHAPTER THREE

# FROM CHILDREN'S THEATRE TO COMMUNITY ARTS 1964-1987
### by Pamela Dellar

In 1961 an imposing new building rose nine storeys high at the end of Queen's Gardens, the former dock which had been turned into a garden. The glass and concrete frontage proclaimed a bright new future for education. Plans were well advanced in the City of Hull for the new system of comprehensive education and, even after the compulsory years of schooling, there were to be innovative liberal studies for many who attended Hull's College of Technology. It was within this framework that drama and theatre found an outlet.

I was invited to set up a drama evening course in the autumn term of 1964, as part of the adult education provision of the College's Department of English and General Studies. One of the department's aims was 'to assist in the promotion of liberal, cultural and artistic pursuits in the City and surrounding areas'. At the time I didn't realise that this was to be the beginning of a long investigation into the role of theatre in the community.

The people who joined the group were mainly school and college students and teachers whose attendance was paid for by the Local Education Authority. We were given rehearsal space on the top floor of the new building overlooking a fairyland view of the City, its lights twinkling at night and its domes outlined against the sky. This why we called one of our first productions *The Land of Green Ginger* because we could just see the tops of the buildings in the street which bears that name.

An article in the *Hull Daily Mail* by Jane Humber (Barbara Duncanson) drew attention to our existence and our performance of three short plays for children in the meeting room of the Central Library — the beginning of a long and friendly relationship with the library service. The headline ran: THERE ARE FAIRIES IN THE COLLEGE OF TECHNOLOGY.

We were not, of course, the first people to provide theatre for children. In response to growing interest, the British Children's Theatre Association had been launched in Leicester in 1959 with the aims: 'to further education for children through drama and the arts of theatre and to encourage the appreciation of dramatic art by and for children'. Like others in the field we were keen to develop a participatory approach, when presenting plays for children, where children could influence the action and take decisions and where the actors worked flexibly through improvisation to devise the plays. Another aim, which seemed to capture the imagination of the public and press, was that of taking the theatre to the children rather than always expecting them to go out to visit the play.

## Methods and Styles

After working for several years in the professional theatre I had taught in the preparatory department of Hull High School for Girls and used drama methods for children derived from practitioners such as Peter Slade, Maise Cobby and Brian Way. So I simply used these methods with adults when devising plays for children. Later I extended the use of principles of primary education to include a system of 'family grouping' wherever possible in the theatre groups. Another firmly established principle was that participation could only be used if it moved the action forward. No 'Oh, no, he isn't! Oh, yes, he, is!' just for the sake of it.

One play that we created this way was *The Explosion* (1969). The story line was simple but there were problems with the participation. Two children find an unexploded bomb on the beach. The wicked king Candelabra has to be overcome to prevent it exploding. This can only be done by the light of a hundred candles. Should we ask the children to imagine the candles?. No, that was an easy way out. After agonising over it for a week I happened to see a craft shop that was selling beeswax sheets for making your own candles. I wrote to the manufacturers asking if they would donate enough beeswax for a week of performances. They sent it by return. Such was the spirit of the Sixties.

So each child in the audience overcame the wicked king by making and lighting a candle (under cast supervision) during the action of the play. It created a beautiful moment and I recall, with pride, one mother who told me that they lit the candle every night at bedtime and it lasted a month!

I started to develop a local history documentary style in 1968 (influenced by Peter Cheeseman's work in Stoke on Trent). Grace Darling had been a childhood heroine of mine and when I realised that the *Forfarshire* had sailed from Hull it was an obvious subject for a play with a particular emphasis on the passengers who boarded in Hull. At the same time a play was devised about smuggling on the East Coast, based on *The Reminiscences of a Revenue Officer* by Lionel J. Felix Hexham. The Watersons, who were just rising to fame as a *capella* folk singers, joined us for the production. Donald Campbell, a founder member of the group, devised a sneaky bit of participation for this as one of the smugglers. He took a note to all our audience — they were our jury — promising them sweets if they voted him not guilty. He got off every time!. We took the play to St. William's Approved School at Market Weighton. There they released the smugglers and retained the hero!

Therapeutic drama was being developed at St. Williams by Brother Marcellus Guyler, whose father, Derek Guyler, was a well-known professional actor. Marcellus came over to our workshop sessions which were now held in the Charterhouse annexe of the College — we'd been moved from our top floor room to make way for the library. He introduced us to the new encounter group methods and touch and trust exercises that had arrived in this country via the Human Potential Movement in the U.S.A. It was a rather introspective time and the effect was to create an incredibly cohesive group. I also included voice training and movement training based on techniques derived from Martha Graham in our workshop sessions. I found Viola Spolen's book, *Improvisation for the Theatre*, was inspirational and a whole term was spent using her methods to develop performances of spontaneous improvisation to audience suggestions.

Of course we always included scripted plays in the year's programme. With Gillian Holtby I adapted a Chinese folk story, *In the Far South West*. It had giants with huge paper maché heads and tiny glove puppet people made out of old nylons by Meta Paterson, whose Merry Go Round Puppets worked within the Theatre For Children.

The Minnikins, as the little people were called, referred constantly to their little red book (this was the time of the Cultural Revolution in China). One phrase, 'Be united, alert, earnest and lively', so impressed John Horsley, a local teacher, that he put it on a banner in his classroom. He also joined the group and became one of our most valued members, writing songs for many productions. We nearly lost Donald Campbell that time, though. He knocked himself out as a tiger jumping into a grand piano in the wings of the new Film Theatre at the Central Library.

Other plays presented included *Gods of the Vikings*, a devised play on the Viking myths, *The Mystery of Cobweb Castle*, *The Owl and the Pussycat Went to See* by David Woods, and Brian Way's *Pinnocchio* which contained a visually remarkable under-the-sea shadow scene created by Meta Paterson using rod puppets and a huge cut-out whale. As one small member of the audience wrote to us afterwards, 'It looked a picture from the back.'

### The Merry Go Round Puppets

Puppetry was always seen as an essential part of theatre for children. We advertised it as a course but had no-one to run it. Then Meta Paterson arrived one evening and found herself teaching the course. This led to the setting up of her professional company, The Merry Go Round Puppets, which was affiliated with the Educational Puppetry Association, the British Puppet and Model Theatre Guild and the Dutch Association of Puppeteers.

She was joined by Pamela Hotham whose talents of vocal mimicry were very effectively used in puppetry, and between them they made an excellent team, visiting schools during the daytime, not only performing but also giving puppetry-making demonstrations and running workshops. We invited Violet Philpotts of the Educational Puppetry Association to visit Hull, and Meta used and developed her methods of making puppets from scrap materials. Egg boxes became dragons, pan scrubs were turned into creepy crawly creatures, and mops were transmogrified into tousle-headed giants. In the 1960's this was innovative although nowadays common at all levels of puppetry.

But Meta also created full-length performances which were presented under more formal conditions. With her small team of puppeteers she presented Hans Anderson's *The Tinder Box* at the Central Library Theatre in 1968. Another very popular programme for young children was *Sam The Sailor* in a double bill with a delightful shadow play *The Mouse In Old Amsterdam*. Meta brought her own culture of childhood from Holland to Hull and received a particularly enthusiastic response from the large Dutch community in the city.

There is a strong tradition of puppetry in Hull. Thomas Sheppard, in his book, *Evolution of the Drama in Hull and District* (1927) refers to a popular marionette theatre in a shed off Malborough Terrace (c.1890). Meta's ambition was to establish a puppet 'cellar' similar to ones she had seen in Holland, and open for exhibitions, weekend and holiday performances. Sadly the ambition was not fulfilled as Meta moved to Kircudbright in Scotland where she established and ran several international puppet festivals. Her contributions to the culture of the city was widely recognised and we never found anyone who could replace her.

### The Venues, the Audiences, the Travelling

The main venues for our productions were schools, play centres, libraries, village halls and church halls, though major theatre productions were held in the Library Theatre and later in Hull Arts Centre/Humberside Theatre (now Spring Street Theatre). Performances were sometimes arranged in schools by the teacher members of the group out of school time but this involved bringing the children back in the evening. It proved a far easier task to arrange performances in play centres.

The play centres had been established during the war as after-school care to assist working mothers. Generally speaking our visits were most welcome though on one occasion we were shocked to receive a letter from a play leader telling us that the Chief Education Officer himself had refused approval for our visit with a new play, a charming adaption of James Thurber's *Many Moons*. With the assistance of Councillor Mrs. Cooper, who had helped to establish the play centres and had fought for their retention after the war, the decision was reversed. The reasons for the refusal were never made clear but were not unconnected with a letter I had written to *The Guardian* concerning the ethics of inviting representatives of Moral Rearmament to speak in schools and present a play at the New Theatre.

The organisation of these visits was an arduous task involving many hours of ringing round, contacting leaders and caretakers and ensuring that everyone knew where to find the venue, for we travelled to every corner of Hull — Bransholme, Bilton, Orchard Park, Gipsyville — often on dark winter nights. Sometimes an actor would get lost and others had to double the part at a moment's notice.

At the end of the school day I would arrive at the venue with Len Watkinson, who was for many years our technical expert. He lit all the plays and created the sound tracks; in fact, it is difficult to imagine how we could have existed without his dedicated help. After locating the power points we then carried in the equipment, blocks, and lights and screens, setting it up in readiness for the cast who would arrive having already done a hard day's work, bringing props and costumes.

A visit to a village was usually a Saturday afternoon treat organised by someone locally, often with tea afterwards. The audience were quietly appreciative because they had parents with them. Not so the play centres. Roland Gift, who later became a famous ' Fine Young Cannibal', recalled a show at Wold Road play centre in 1974 when 'there were about three hundred kids there all shouting'. One of the problems was that the playleaders were so glad of a rest that they tended to send all the children in, regardless of age or numbers, until we firmly made a number restriction. Yet many of our actor/teachers said they liked the play centres best. They felt the audience was more of a challenge. The saddest little performances were the ones taken into the hospitals where we had to adjust to a small number of very quiet children on the ward.

So by 1970, in the College, although only employed for four of five hours a week, I had been instrumental in developing a student theatre group; the Theatre for Children; a Saturday morning junior drama workshop; a series of visiting lectures including John Hodgson, Dorothy Heathcote, Derek Bowskill; and a *Jackanory* story and drama club at the Central Library on Saturday afternoons.

## A Community Play 1974

By 1973 we were based in a back room in the Park Street annexe of the College, having been moved from the Charterhouse annexe to make way for marine engineers. We were allowed to create a small studio in the former Victorian house and we had access to other rooms so that groups could rehearse all over the building. Props were stored in the attics. It was also conveniently situated near the Arts Centre which had opened in 1970; in 1992 it is called Spring Street Theatre and is the base for Hull Truck. I was the secretary of the Arts Centre appeal group from its inception in 1963 and it was gratifying to see it working at last, although in a much smaller form than originally intended.

One evening we were sharing ideas about our next project when Chris Johnson said, 'What about James Acland?' I gasped with delight. 'Are you really interested? It'd be a tremendous amount of hard work.' The idea had been hovering around my mind for several years, ever since one summer Dr. Joyce Bellamy, the local historian, had allowed me to search the Meadley Newspaper Archive at the University. It was there that I came across riots in Hull in the early 1830's and their connection with James Acland, the publisher of a radical newspaper called *Hull Portfolio*.

To start with we set up a research group. At one point a discussion arose on whether to keep to the actual words used at the time or to invent new dialogue. We agreed to keep entirely to documentary material and this provided us with a cohesive discipline. It was also decided that the Commission into Municipal Corporations should provide the basic framework, with flashbacks to the topics raised during the inquiry. Eventually I wrote it up and provided links. The title *A Farthing For Public Opinion* was taken from the ferry trial where Acland was fined a farthing for running his ferry, the *Public Opinion*, which plied between Hull and Barton, in opposition to the Corporation's own ferry monopoly.

Now it so happened that 1974 was the year of local government re-organisation (when the County of Humberside was created and the East Riding of Yorkshire ceased to exist!) so, quite by chance, our play proved particularly topical. It was also a time when corruption had been exposed in Newcastle, and councils were very sensitive. I received a phone call from Leo Schultz, the leader of the City Council. What were we doing? There was no corruption in Hull. If this was the sort of thing we were putting on at the Arts Centre it certainly wouldn't get his support!. In vain I protested our innocent intention. After all, it was over a 100 years ago.

The *Hull Daily Mail* headline read 'PLAY SHOWS OLD HULL A CORRUPT CITY'. The newly formed Humberside County Council gave us a grant.

It packed out the Arts Centre (now renamed Humberside Theatre). Over 50 people took part, including the East Riding yeomanry band. A replica of the statue of King Billy (superbly designed by Alan Davis, who was later to make a name for himself as a designer with Yorkshire T.V.) dominated the stage. A programme note by Philip Judd read, 'Compared with other cities the incidents in Hull were relatively mild. But Hull is a good example of a town in which the latent dissatisfaction could easily be roused by one man, James Acland.' We researched it. We wrote it. We acted it. We suffered for it — and it was about our own town. It was several years later that Anne

Jellicoe (author of *Community Plays*, 1987), identified the genre as the 'community play'. Anne and I were contemporaries at the Central School of Drama just after the war. She wrote plays and directed in London before settling in rural Dorset. I worked in travelling theatre and settled in a northern industrial town. Yet eventually we both found commitment and a professional outlet in community theatre. We seem to share a common philosophy — if nothing's happening you make it happen, and a way to make it happen is to make a play.

### Celebratory and Folk Events

Over the years I devised a number of outdoor events. The first of these was at Burton Constable Hall in 1967. I had visited and admired the 18th-century stable block, designed by Thomas Lightoler, and so, nothing daunted, rang up to discuss the idea of an event. I was invited to call and was greeted at the side door of the hall by a young woman, quite tall with dark hair and a direct open manner. This was Gaye Chichester Constable. She took me through a dark passage to a comfortable sitting room with a huge log fire burning in a great stone fireplace and a long-haired dachshund snoozing on the velvet sofa. After a few minutes a bookcase on the wall opened like a door and John Chichester Constable joined us. We discussed the idea and it grew into a Country Revel. I contacted lots of groups and in particular Kathy Mitchell, who was the much loved and enthusiastic representative of the English Folk Dance and Song Society. The final event was held on Midsummer Eve and included jigs, drolls, quips and quidities, ballads, jests and song, chivalrie (well, archery actually); routs and roundelays, a mumming play and an evening barn dance. Our country games consisted of marrow dangling and rhubarb thrashing — a vicious game where the aim is to sit on a beer barrel trying to hit your opponent on the head with a stick of rhubarb and drinking a pint of cider between each blow! Gaye and John were delighted by the crowds who turned up. They had only recently inherited the rather crumbling mansion and were keen to make local contacts. The Revels were repeated the following two years.

I was also involved with organising celebrations in Hull's Market Place. The first was to commemorate the centenary of Hull Trinity House Navigation School, the second to assist the Holy Trinity Church Restoration Appeal. E. R. Eddon, the Headmaster of Trinity House, was the chairman for both events and John Munday and I worked closely together to organise the second. The *Hull Play of Noah* was performed at both events.

Activities had now changed direction from the earlier Theatre For Children and so it was agreed to rename the group as the Community Theatre Workshop. We were not professional, although some professionals worked with us, training sessions were an important feature (hence the use of the word 'workshop'), and we were always open to anyone who wanted to come.

But things were not going well at the College of Technology which supported these activities. In 1975 economies were being made and the reorganisation into the Colleges of Higher and Further Education was taking place. There was a scramble for jobs and some full-timers were interested in the teaching hours of the Community Theatre Workshop.

We were working on the play, *Charlie Peace*, by the docker playwright Dave Marson. A previous play of his, *Fall In And Follow Me*, about the 1911 school children's strikes, had received national acclaim. But it had been criticised locally for its 'bad language'. A complete script was demanded by the College. I was unable to provide one as the play was still being written. Things became unpleasant and finally I was asked to give a date for the 'termination of your Thursday evening class'.

Temporarily we were housed, first by the College of Art, then by Hull Truck in High Street. There we devised *The Fabulous Adventures of Baron Von Grumpelfink*. In the summer, with Jeanne Oldfield, I set up a Centre for Performing Arts in an old deserted school in Fountain Road. Then I was invited by John Stoddart, the new Principal of the College of Higher Education, to take the Community Theatre Workshop into the College as the core of their new community arts courses. Jeanne Oldfield came as well to offer dance and movement and John Munday was officially attached to the course although he had already worked with us voluntarily for several years.

Jeanne had worked professionally with Brian Way's Children's Theatre Company after training at the Rose Bruford School of Drama. On returning to teach in Hull she worked as a volunteer with the Theatre For Children Group and then went to study Laban based dance at the Art of Movement studio.

John Munday brought to the College and the courses his own expertise in design, puppetry and participatory theatre. He had worked with puppets on Australian T.V. before coming to England where he was employed by Nathans, the theatrical costumiers. He then studied educational drama at Trent Park College and from there went to Bournemouth drama centre where he learned the techniques of promenade theatre which he used and developed in most of his productions. It was an innovative and popular style. He also loved the medieval theatre and directed several plays of the period including the *Hull Play of Noah* and *The Castle of Perseverance*, which was staged in Beverley Market Place and Beverley Minster with the actors moving amongst the spectators in bright costumes which he designed and made himself. His designs for the Theatre for Children were a delight. John was a popular and often inspirational director and teacher with the unique gift of being able to enter into the child's world of fantasy and play.

Everyone loved the new accommodation in the College of Higher

Education, including Roland Gift, who wrote in his G.C.E. project in 1977: 'As far as facilities go this is by far the best. The main hall is where we meet and do most of our rehearsing. It has a stage with lights and a large seating area, there is also a property cum dressing room leading off from the stage. We can book the video and sound studios. There are craft rooms where people can work with paint, wood, clay and weaving. We are currently working on a production based around the statues of Hull. This is partly to do with it being the Queen's Silver Jubilee year, but is more along the lines of anti-Jubilee celebrations. We are taking stories behind the statues and acting them out and what happened to cause the statues to be erected.'

We all felt that the future of the Community Theatre Workshop was assured. Two years later, in the summer of 1979 and with no warning, Humberside County Council closed down all adult and continuing education courses for the coming year.

The damage was immediate and lasting. All over Humberside part-time adult tutors were thrown out of work, most of them women. Amongst them of course were Jeanne Oldfield and myself. The dedicated group who had been with the Community Theatre Workshop since its early days stayed together as an independent drama group, with the assistance of John Munday, to complete a local history play they had devised and written about the rural East Riding in the 19th century. It was called *Only A Man Labouring*. They have remained together ever since, often working in promenade style on plays for children and retaining the name Hull Community Theatre. It had after all become a way of life.

### The Art College Theatre Group 1968-1979

Art Colleges in Yorkshire developed a special sort of theatrical energy in the 1970s. It is only possible to describe briefly what happened in Hull and indicate how it influenced the development of community arts in the city. In 1968 I was invited to contribute to the complementary studies programme of Hull College of Art by providing a drama and theatre studies option on one morning each week. From a group of about 15 students this eventually grew until nearly half the college was involved in the Art College Theatre Group.

We were based in the original Art College building, designed in 1904 by E. A. Rickards. It has an elegant entrance hall and staircase and, on the ground floor, a large room with pillars and a stage. This room had been used as a theatre since the 1930s when Sam Hemming became the College Principal and staged a number of productions there. It was here that the theatre group staged its first productions.

By 1973, with several productions behind us of plays by Ayckbourn, Stoppard and Halliwell, I chose to direct the *Lysistrata* of Aristophanes. The play contained all the elements of theatrical freedom that the times called for but at the dress rehearsal the end lacked visual excitement until I suddenly came up with the idea for a wonderful final scene in which a young bare-breasted goddess was carried in covered in gold make-up (shades of James Bond's *Goldfinger!*) and twirling aloft under a strobe light. We took the play to the Ferens Art Gallery and performed it in the 'centre court', a spacious central space reflected by a circular balcony above — the first time a play has been presented in that setting. This was the year that Hull Truck presented *Children Of The Lost Planet* and, after seeing the performance at the Arts Centre, I asked Mike Bradwell to bring the production into the Art College. We were now based on the top floor and poor Hull Truck had to carry their equipment up the three flights of the wonderful curving staircase which is a feature of the building. After the performance, Peter Hammond, the lecturer in charge of History of Art and Complementary Studies, invited Mike to join the team of visiting tutors. This created a trio of tutors attached to the theatre group as Jeanne Oldfield also joined us as dance and movement tutor.

Our first joint production was the *Marat/Sade* by Peter Weiss. It proved an excellent piece of theatre for three directors. Mike coached the protagonists, I worked on the large group scenes and Jeanne choreographed the movement sequences. A student, John Richardson, was the musical director. It was presented to packed audiences at the Ferens Gallery where Mike created an institutional atmosphere by scrubbing the marble hall with disinfectant, then closing the doors with an ominous clang as the 'mental patients straggled in 'Poor Old Marat ... we want our revolution NOW.'

After *Marat/Sade* the spirit of anarchy was released. Half the college wanted to join the theatre group. Events and happenings were the rage and I recall taking a group of students, with their Fine Art tutor, to 'levitate the customs house' as a conceptual art project whilst the occupants leaned anxiously from the windows lest we should succeed. The event was interrupted by the police after a flag, placed on a fountain, had caused local fears that the student terror was about to break loose in Hull.

Each week we held drama workshops in our top floor room and for a while toyed with the idea of a play about Amy Johnson, the greatly admired Hull heroine. At every point where Amy landed she was to become involved with scenes and stars from the Thirties' films. It got beyond us and I passed the idea on to Richard Green who created a musical about Amy for his newly formed Northern Theatre Company.

We discussed Dada and Surrealism, the Bauhaus and the performance experiments at Black Mountain College and eventually did a Charivari on the staircase. Visual ideas proliferated. A body fell down the stairwell, a room was filled with criss-crossed string and dry ice; black light enveloped 'the still unravished brides of quietness' (Jeanne's dancers), and a stripper dressed in black under her clothes stripped off everything under a strobe light to reveal ... nothing.

Students from the School of Architecture staged a happening and arrived costumed as police. One lecturer, recently returned from the U.S.A., rushed forward protectively, 'Don't worry. I'll deal with the pigs!' His fury knew no bounds when he discovered the event was based on a recent Bunuel movie. The audience milled up and down the stair well. Chaos reigned. It was great!

What next? The students grew restless. They wanted to create their own thing. Not a play, but like it. Not a happening. 'Why don't you get on with it?'said Mike. They set up a tea dance in a semi-derelict village hall in Marfleet. The village had been swamped years ago by factories, the docks and the prison, but a tiny, tiny bit remains — an old farmhouse, a church and a village hall. Students and staff of the college turned out in force, dressed in stripey blazers, white flannels, voile dresses. We ate cucumber sandwiches, danced to cracked 78's and played games. Richard Lanham went off to work with Welfare State International, the international performance group whose founders John and Sue Fox both come from Hull. This was after Richard attempted to fly across the Humber by kite. He came back from Welfare State breathing fire, and the theatre group joined him at a fire dragon event in Fountain Road where all the houses were being demolished to make way for a new housing estate. An improvised play was demanded — after all, this was Mike's speciality. Hull Truck was doing well.

So Mike agreed, with some reluctance, for how was it possible to reach the depth of improvisation needed to produce a play in only one session a week? Each person had to study a character who interested them and bring it to rehearsal. Mike placed them in groups together, decided where they were and scenes were developed. The theme was Hull at night. The scenes were linked by a strange character called Mad John, based on a man who lived in an old car on Hessle foreshore and used to rush out and wave at the trains as they went past, and the play was given the title *Mad John and the Greasy Sprinter*. It was presented at Hull Arts Centre/Humberside Theatre as part of an Arts Week, organised by me in March, 1975. Other events in the week, all presented by college students, were dance, a writers' workshop, music improvisation, video drama, puppets, collage, photoplay, exhibitions, rubbish arrangements, graffiti. Eric Goulden (who was later known in the pop world as Reckless Eric) was a student at the College and heavily involved in rubbish. He collected this from Hessle foreshore, arriving with a pram load at Paragon Station to be interviewed by Radio Humberside and then continuing to the theatre where he created a rubbish arrangement. The reception was mixed. Mike was working on the latest Hull Truck play and involved in video work with the students. We had to go across to Leeds Polytechnic for this as there was no equipment in the College. Two of the students who made a very interesting video later went on to join the National Theatre — Lynn in the box office and Alan in the

bookshop. But Hull Truck was now needing all Mike's attention. He was beginning to tire of tutoring in the college and the stop-go policies regarding the theatre group. Finally, after a row about the caretaker who had walked into a rehearsal, he left. Jeanne and I continued, still reeling from the after-effects. It had been an exhilarating and never to be forgotten experience, working with Mike Bradwell and I shall always be grateful to him for teaching me a lot. I went on to direct Genet's *The Maids*, *The Sea* by Edward Bond and finally Wedekind's *Lulu*, all presented at Humberside Theatre. Then a new head of Fine Art arrived. He favoured performance art and not performing arts, an important distinction not always appreciated outside the world of fine art. Changes took place. Complementary Studies disappeared. So did the Art College Theatre Group (1979).

In concluding this whole section on the theatre work within the colleges it is important to recognise the contribution of the members of staff concerned with educational development there at the time: Peter Hammond at the College of Art, D. I. Davies at the College of Technology, John Stoddart, the director of the College of Higher Education, and Graham Worthington, the Assistant Director. They had the vision and commitment to the principles of a liberal education. They helped to make things possible.

So what happened next?. The Faculty of Art and Design within the College of Higher Education continued to develop performance art. In 1982 a group of six graduates formed the Open Performance Group. In 1984 they joined with other artists in establishing Hull Time Based Arts which included experimental film, video and music. This group was responsible for the spectacular Tidal Barrier Event for Hull Festival, a futuristic presentation with music by John Stead and movement designed by Karen Rann. This event was the first of many which helped to lead the arts in the City forward into the last decade of the twentieth century.

Other developments influenced by the work at the College of Art and directly connected with the Community Theatre Workshop were The Women's Theatre Group and Outreach Community /Arts ...


## OUTREACH COMMUNITY ARTS 1979-1987

The Council of Europe was created in the years of rebuilding after the war, to act as a moral force in Europe, aiming to express aspirations, ideals and expertise of member countries. In the mid-1970s its council for cultural co-operation focused attention on the democratisation of culture, including access to the arts. There was concern amongst some practitioners that the arts reflected the culture of the minority who had the money to spend and the education to appreciate and participate. It was also noted that large urban populations were losing a sense of community and it was suggested that the arts could provide the opportunity for people to work together creatively, in groups, thereby expressing their interests and needs.

A series of symposia held by the Council included such topics as 'Towards Cultural Democracy', 'Cultural Policy in Towns', and 'The Role of the Animateur'. The term *animateur* may need definition as it is difficult to find the English equivalent for the French word. The simplest seeing it as an individual or group who 'get things going' or, as one member of a symposium put it, 'a disturber of pleasant routines'. Pierre Moulinier, voicing some of the Council's findings (1978) said, 'The ideal would of course be for those animateurs to stem from the local population in order to understand it and fully express its outlook.' The aim of animateurs in the context of the arts had been recognised by the Arts Council of Great Britain in its report on Community Arts (1974).

Meanwhile, at the College of Higher Education in Hull, in a paper on adult and continuing education, Peter Adamson had presented the idea of 'outreach' workers whose brief would be to work outside the formal educational establishment, in other words a similar concept to that of the 'animateur'.

In the late 1970s the growing problem of unemployment was leading to the creation of employment schemes by the Manpower Services Commission. These included the Special Temporary Employment Programme (S.T.E.P) for those over the age of 19. These jobs lasted only for one year and were sponsored by organisations who were re-imbursed by the M.S.C. for wages, national insurance and a per capita allowance for each employee.

All this contributed to the thinking behind a proposal which I presented to the College of Higher Education for the setting up of a community arts team.

The team was seen as an Outreach project, drawing people into the College's community arts courses and providing arts support for groups in the community at large. The work of the Community Theatre Workshop provided the experimental basis for the proposal which was presented in September, 1978, although final approvals delayed the start until the following year. In 1979 the Manpower Services Commission agreed to support the project as follows:

| Salaries | £29,283.48 |
| Per capita | £2,400.00 |
| | £31,683.48 |

Hull College of Higher Education agreed to sponsor the project and provide funding of £4,700, less any income generated by the scheme. This did not include the hidden cost of administrative back-up and accommodation but did include training and supervision costs. One of the aims was undermined when the L.E.A. closed down all the College's community arts courses just as the project was established.

The objectives, which were rather over-ambitious, were to:
1. take the arts outside normal venues in order to make them more accessible.
2. provide facilities and expertise to help people develop their own creative skills.
3. provide opportunities for people to work together creatively in order to express their own ideas and concerns.
4. assist a sense of community by responding to a need for celebration.
5. encourage emergent art forms within popular culture.

The first project was at Spurn Point. The College had a field centre there. A wonderful place where the old lighthouse keeper's cottages nestled inside a high brick rotunda in which the original Smeaton lighthouse used to stand. Beyond the walls the North Sea was gradually eroding the dunes and on the horizon boats queued up waiting for pilots to lead them down the treacherous channels of the Humber estuary. At the very end of the promontary stands an isolated group of houses where the lifeboat men and their families live, surrounded by the sea, the sand and the buckthorn. Superb for children one would think, but not so, as we discovered one summer. With the Community Theatre Workshop we had made a Super 8 movie with the children and they had complained about having no where to play. The sea was not to be trusted and the old army pill boxes had tempting tunnels which could collapse.

So the community arts team, based in the field centre, discussed the needs and helped to create a playground. With the children they painted a mural of a crowd at a stadium and then helped to obtain play equipment donated by B.P. Chemicals. This was followed up by a season of films provided by Hull Film Society who won a prize for the project and were then able to donate film projection equipment for use in the community centre. Although this project was in no way theatrical it is mentioned here because it set out useful guidelines that were applied to most projects thereafter.

**Some Performance Based Projects**

These included puppet shows, mime projects with deaf children, music revues for the elderly, the handicapped and mentally ill, and fire festivals.

The first of these fire festivals was held in Fountain Road. In 1978 I had discussed our proposals with the Lincolnshire and Humberside Arts Association. Shortly afterwards they had placed their own community arts worker, Jeannie Posnett, in a community centre in Fountain road with little in the way of resources or support. They called this their Hull community arts project. We suggested a fire festival for bonfire night, as a joint venture, with Jeannie running mask making workshops at the community centre and the Outreach team organising a torchlight procession, the bonfire and performance based on the theme of Earth, Air, Fire and water. Jo Digger, who had already worked with fire as a performance medium, led the project and herself provided a spectacular fire breathing performance. This was the first of four fire festivals devised by Outreach Community Arts. The second was more closely involved with the local community of North Bransholme.

Bransholme is a huge housing estate originally planned as a satellite town for Hull but left with few amenities when the new-town scheme was jettisoned. Brian Petch, a local councillor, who has a keen interest in community arts, helped to create the contact with the North Bransholme community centre. Here we ran performance and craft workshops and also went into local schools. At the community centre arguments raged on. When I showed concern at this they looked at me with amazement. 'But we always argue — we like it — it shows that we get on.'

The result was an incredible torchlight procession of about 700 people round the estate. We'd been round telling people it was going to happen, knocking on doors. 'What is it?' cried a voice through the keyhole. We explained about the festival. The latches were lifted: 'I thought it were them kids again.'

The bonfire was guarded overnight by the Scouts. Someone sat up in the community centre to guard the fireworks. On the night, two huge puppets looking remarkably like Maggie Thatcher and Ronnie Reagan were consigned to the flames. A children's roundabout swung into action. Sausage rolls, cans of fizzy and cups of tea were sold in the community centre. The dancing started and was brought to an abrupt halt.

'Out!' said the committee chairman. 'Out!'

'Why?'

'They're playing up again, those kids. Always spoil it for themselves.'

Docilely everyone packed up and left. All agreed it had been a great occasion and worth it, even if it hadn't raised a lot of money for the centre. We went back to show the video. It certainly looked spectacular. It had been on Y.T.V. news as well (they had also sponsored it) so it must have been good! We never had a single accident at the festivals that I can remember. By creating a performance ritual of the event it helped to give an appreciation of the power of fire. Perhaps, too, it represented an outside force which helped to draw the community together. Bonfire night in Hull is one of the great events of the year, falling as it does hard on the heels of Hull Fair.

Another traditional event was a Plough Monday play which the team took out into Holderness without warning, in the manner of the original 'plough stots'. They arrived at Hedon school and took the children onto the green by the church, then continued on to Thorngumbald, Patrington, Skirlaugh and Roos. There was a thin layer of snow on the ground and one could truly feel the unique solitude of Holderness.

*The Worm of Wincolmlee* on the other hand was far from traditional, although based on the traditional theme of the Lampton worm. It travelled down Whitefriargate to celebrate the winter solstice after being assembled at the Ferens Art Gallery. Someone recited a lengthy poem whilst St. Hugh of Wincolmlee (Hugh Whitaker) challenged and slaughtered it. It was of course restored to life whereupon everyone repaired to the nearest public house for carols and refreshment. Wincolmlee itself is the winding road alongside the dirty and industrialised part of the River Hull from whence the City takes its name.

For Outreach the summer brought many outdoor events including one unforgettable performance of a Silly Olympics in a field of cow pats near Driffield with the Driffield Navigational Society.

Alongside all this were the on-going arts workshops at day centres, youth centres and intermediate treatment centres. Mural projects were held with the patients in all types of hospitals; puppet shows for children and in pubs; photography and video workshops. Charlie Arnold was surprised one day when a white witch arrived, glowing in trailing garments to video record her poems at one of his open workshop sessions. Life was always full of surprises.

## The End Of The Team

Under the terms of the Special Temporary Employment Programme, personnel had to change at the end of a year's work and a new working pattern had to be drawn to fit the skills of a new team. It was disheartening. The Calouste Gulbenkian Foundation, recognising the problems, gave me a grant to enable me to seek ways of placing the work on a more permanent basis. With the help of students of the School of Architecture I prepared an application to the Inner Area Programme to turn our base into an Arts Resource Centre with a supporting group of arts workers. The application for the arts resource centre was approved but I was unable to find a source of funding for the community arts team. It disbanded in April, 1982.

## The Arts Resource Centre

Before it disbanded the arts team had moved into the redundant primary school, which was to become the Arts Resource Centre on Northumberland Avenue, on a cold October day in 1980. It was damp, with antique radiators, an ill-lit vestibule, a large hall, some sinks and a small room where we held meetings huddled over a gas fire. Outside was a walled playground. On one side some almshouses (where we gradually made some close friends), and on the other side Community Industry in another larger Victorian building. At the rear was a piece of waste ground, the site of a drain which, along with many such water courses, had been filled in by the Council in the 1960s and left untended since. Beyond this there was an adult education centre in prefabs and another Victorian school for children with learning difficulties. To the east, corn oil and paint factories filled the air with musty smells on windless days and to the west stood the new housing estate in Fountain Road.

While the renovations were being completed we moved to an old school in Somerset Street. It was a bleak time. The windows of the school were boarded up and we were sharing the premises with the City Council's mural and mosaic project — a fine white choking dust filled the air from the chipping of the tiles. I was not well and suffering a deep personal bereavement. The windowless building seems to symbolise the agony of that time.

In the Spring of 1983 we moved back to the building which was now restored and redesigned by A.B.C. community architects. Bright colours, reds and yellows greeted us as we unloaded our equipment through the doors. A red spiral staircase led us to a new mezzanine floor above the circulation area. The hall, now a dance and drama studio, was complete with dance mirrors, a dance bar and a viewing gallery. In the next phase of the building programme an outside studio was added for silk screen and poster printing and later still a back room converted into a film and video studio. There was also a photography dark room and office space.

So here we were with a purpose-made building but no arts team. Lesley Garry as administrator and myself as director and development officer, together with Norman the caretaker, represented the sum total of staffing. The housing estate nearby was where the two Lincolnshire and Humberside Arts workers were based. As they also received funding from the Inner Area Programme it seemed logical for them to move to the Arts Resource Centre.

Together we set up workshops in dance, film, video, drama, poster printing, writing and photography, offering training facilities to community groups, voluntary organisations and the public at large. We stretched our own personal resources to the limit. Jeannie Posnett ran a highly successful poster print workshop, an unemployed theatre group and a drama group for the local children.

I devised several projects linked to the local community. One of these, the Martinmas Folk Fair, lasted throughout a November weekend and established a community garden on the site of the filled in drain.

Martinmas was a traditional time of the year for seeking work and the existing climate of unemployment linked with this theme. A country crafts fair was followed by an evening barn dance led by the Green Ginger band and the Chilean Folk Group, Melinka, who gave so much to Hull's culture for over a decade before they returned to Chile in 1990. The following day the Hull Architecture workshop organised a tree planting event called 'Daisy Roots and Dirty Boots'. In all 84 trees and 40 shrubs were planted after the Holderness Morris Men had firmly prepared the ground by dancing on it to make things grow.

Another event, devised in co-operation with Councillor Brian Petch, took place on Victoria Pier. This was originally intended as a farewell to the Humber Ferry when the Humber Bridge opened. The day dawned bright and sunny and Brian Petch was up at 6 o'clock sweeping the street before rushing off to robe himself for the corporate procession. The Lord Mayor processed in a vintage car, provided by the museum, to the pier where a service was held for National Sea Sunday and thereafter the stalls opened and the celebrations began, including a reconstruction of Houdini's escape from a sack thrown into the muddy waters of the Humber. Thousands turned up, many of them dressed in Edwardian costumes. It was very popular and has continued to this very day although now it is held in Queen's Gardens and some of the ceremony has been lost. It is called the Edwardian Sunday.

## People Make Place

This title was used by Hull Architecture workshop for their own own environmental projects but it is equally applicable to the Arts Resource Centre and incidentally has been adapted as the title of this book.

The poet Douglas Dunn called Hull 'a rumoured city', and, sure enough, it soon got round that the Outreach Arts Centre was a friendly place where you could keep warm and try your hand at all sorts of activities. People came from all over the City, amongst them some outstanding personalities.

Cliff's family came from Fountain Road but he now lived on North Hull Estate. He attended regularly after finding a deep enthusiasm for drama. He used to tell his family he was going to his club. He was disabled and consequently unemployed and had done an Elvis Presley act in his youth. He appeared in many of the productions of the Act One Theatre Workshop (alternative and community theatre). An outstanding production was devised by Jedd, Dave and Cliff. Ferocious arguments raged on the mezzanine whilst we quaked beneath. They all had an experience to relate of being in prison, even if only briefly, and their play provided a revealing insight into prison conditions. It was critical, funny and moving. It was taken to many local venues and Jedd received a best actor award at a local drama festival for his portrayal of the central character. Anna Maria was another regular attender for a time and worked her way through from being a school cleaner to obtaining an A'Level in Theatre Studies and publishing her own book of poems.

With the County Council's music therapist, Clare Edwards, we set up an entertainments unit to take round to the elderly. Later we went on to develop a reminiscence threatre group with material collected by Clare during her day-to-day work in homes for the elderly. This was greatly appreciated especially when we included local comment on such things as using Reckitt's Blue on wash day. Many of our audience had been on the

Reckitt's production line filling those little blue bags to banish the wash-day blues!

I discovered that many people who came to the centre rarely had the opportunity to get out into the countryside or to visit other towns. One trip was organised by Dave Batty in the Outreach mini-bus to visit the site of a medieval village in the Wolds and Rievaulx Abbey in North Yorkshire, where some of the company performed scenes from Shakespeare, just for ourselves and one or two incredulous tourists. Jeannie Posnett took the unemployed theatre group to a theatre festival in London and several visits were made to the photography museum in Bradford. We even had one trip in search of the other end of 'the Barmy drain'. It was an interesting town and country experience. The murky waters of the Barmston Drain flow through Fountain Road. The other end flows into the sea at the little village of Barmston.

## Re-organisation

In 1986, after rigorous inspection and debate, Humberside County Council decided to accept Outreach Community Arts as a statutory adult education provision in Hull and Lincolnshire, and Humberside Arts agreed to fund the Outreach project directly. Tony Hales was appointed to work in film, video and photography. Jackie Selby was already providing invaluable clerical and reception support. With only a year or so to go to my retirement I stayed on as the drama worker. By this time the following drama groups were based at the resource centre or received our assistance.

| | |
|---|---|
| Evergreen Reminiscence Theatre — | takes music theatre to the elderly. |
| Community Entertainments Unit — | takes entertainment to hospitals. |
| P.R.A.T.S. Players | — disabled theatre group |
| Why Not Theatre Co. | — unemployed theatre group |
| Taboo Theatre Co. | — a young people's theatre group. |
| Strawberry Walkers. | — women's theatre group |
| Modicum Theatre. | — unemployed theatre group |
| Act One Theatre Workshop. | — drama training workshop |
| Riff Raff Theatre. | — unemployed theatre group |
| Children's drama group. | |
| Splash Theatre Co. | — professional theatre group specializing in youth theatre work. |
| Theatrelink. | — a link group for play productions |
| Capercailles Dance Co. — | |
| operation. | — a contemporary dance workshop. |

I also organised drama workshops with visiting professionals, and a Peace Play Festival. Two writers' weekends produced two editions of a publication called *Talking Writing* edited by Audrey Dunne.

The setting-up of a theatre group for people with disabilities was very rewarding. A letter had arrived at Outreach from the Community Care team asking for a drama workshop. I soon discovered that they wanted to do a play. We chose the *Wizard of Oz*. Angela, a lovely bright-eyed young women whose disability restricted her to a wheelchair, played Dorothy and led her fellow actors down the yellow brick road. They puffed and struggled after her, complaining about the uneven surface, the curb, the difficulty of moving fast. Ron Walker's walking frame became part of his costume as scarecrow. 'Not again!' he moaned as they set off once more down the yellow brick road.

'We can't learn the words!' they howled.

'Busk it!' I bellowed, and then I would tell the story of a scene and we improvised it. Then they learnt it. No problem!. Everyone helped paint the backcloth, designed by Tim, a student from the School of Architecture. Ron grabbed a paintbrush in his mouth. Tracy painted with her feet. Annette, who is partially sighted, painted as directed and so we moved forward to the first night. I ranted and raged and told them they were useless. They assured me they loved it. They said they felt they were being treated like real people, and anyway it showed I cared.

We all cared, and when, on the first night, the audience stamped and cheered and clapped and wouldn't let them go, we were all enthralled by the experience of success.

In the middle of the second production, loosely based on Voltaire's *Candide*, I reached my 60th birthday, and had expressed my wish to retire when my work commitments were completed. The Divisional Principal of adult education did not renew my contract or find a replacement drama worker. It was a stupidly insensitive attempt to save money and it created an uproar, particularly from supporters of the PRATS PLAYERS (this stood for Physically Restricted Amateur Theatre Society and was chosen by the group; they later changed the name to the Freewheel Theatre Co). Eventually Max Bird, the chairman of the education committee, intervened and I was able to complete the production but there was still no replacement drama worker at the centre. People wrote to the papers, contacted their M.P.s and wrote to the Council.

Looking back I think the greatest loss to community arts in Hull was when the arts team ceased to exist. Our young and inexperienced team only scratched the surface of the possibilities. Often they lacked confidence and found criticism hard to deal with, especially from other practitioners who had a narrower view of community arts. Increasingly they were discovering the potential of inter-agency policies, working with the youth service, the community care team, intermediate treatment centres and with people who deserve to benefit from arts subsidies as much as the regular attenders at theatres and galleries, but they were also aware of the energy and commitment experienced when working on large scale projects with community groups.

Meanwhile in 1991 Outreach provides us with a little model for the future. It has been re-named Artworks and offers a wide range of creative activities with particular emphasis on media skills. Children's murals brighten the walls of the playground and in the community garden the trees grow taller.

# CHAPTER FOUR

# FREEWHEEL... theatre for the disabled 1987-1990
### by Jenny Foreman

When I joined Freewheel Theatre Company in 1987 and took on the role of Artistic Director, paid on a four-hour-a week Adult Education contract, I suspected that I faced a somewhat different challenge. What I didn't realise was that this work would be the dominant factor in my life for the following two years. Freewheel was a group of about 15 long-term unemployed, physically disabled and able-bodied adults with a wide range of intellectual, emotional and physical characteristics. The core of the company was made up of alert and intelligent, wheelchair-bound adults who were reliant on others to take them anywhere and, literally, everywhere. As a group, we had one characteristic in common and that was a passionate desire for theatre and performance.

If, as it is often said, theatre reflects life — and holds a mirror up to nature, then, like nature it must be composed of highly varied elements. Too often, theatre groups are formed which have mutual agreement as their basis and audiences are presented with a closed, soft-centred view of the world. However, a group which doesn't have an accepted norm throws into sharp focus the differences between people, and Freewheel depended and thrived on the diversity of its members. For many of them life was a struggle to cope, not only financially, but with the most basic of daily routines, such as dressing or going to the toilet, let alone performing in a full scale play. Perhaps this is why I have never known a group of people who had a stronger or more positive self-image. Also, they had no compunction when it came to saying exactly what they thought — as I frequently and painfully discovered.

My initial aim was to persuade the group to change their name. P.R.A.T.S. had been thought of by one of the first members of the group and it was meant to be 'cocking a snook' at those people who used derisory terms to describe disabled people. However, I was aware that it wasn't exactly a name which fell comfortably from the lips of administrators and officers of prospective funding bodies, such as local businesses and arts organisations. It was also a little off-putting for publicity, so, after, a heated debate and the risk of a few hurt feelings, we agreed to change it. I asked for suggestions and the only one remotely repeatable was Freewheel. This name seemed to fit in rather nicely with the other local names in theatre companies, such as Hull Truck and Remould, as it kept to the theme of transport. Also, this was our pre-mini bus era, and so transport was a major time-consuming anxiety of ours.

P.R.A.T.S. began with high ideals. It was never formed as a performing arts group with a therapeutic goal, or as a special needs group showing plays to other special needs groups. The aims were never the traditional ones based on the medical or administrative view that disability results in inability and dependency and requires curing and caring services only. From the beginning the group involved able-bodied people as well as disabled people and, when I joined the group, it was made quite clear to me that their aims were educational and artistic and based on the belief that the disabled should be free to mix with anyone, and be free to learn and free to develop as artists in their own right. As it turned out this was asking a very great deal and I learned the hard way that society and the post-compulsory education system neither recognise nor seek to respond to that demand.

Once the new name was settled, my second move was to build up a team of people to work with. During the first, introductory meeting I was told that all the disabled and able-bodied members of the group wanted to act. They wanted, above anything else, to be performers, and they were not keen to become involved in the other aspects of play-making, such as publicity, set, props, costume, and all the administrative side. By the end of my first proper workshop with the group, when half of them failed to arrive because of late transport which necessitated my going off to collect them in my car, it did occur to me that, perhaps, I had bitten off more than I could chew. The only answer was to find funding to employ some one else to help. Fortunately, Alan Bond, then the Drama Officer, at what was Lincolnshire and Humberside Arts, offered a modest fee for a production assistant, and I found a recent Hull University Drama graduate, Debbie Howe, who was keen to take this on. Next, by some miracle, Carol Parkinson turned up and volunteered to sort out the transport nightmare and financial accounts. So, we were off.

By September, 1988, Freewheel Theatre Company had put on a totally integrated, disabled and able-bodied production of Shakespeare's play, *The Tempest*, at Spring Street Theatre and at the Hull University Gulbenkian Studio Theatre. It took me a month to adapt the play for the group before we could start to rehearse, but it was worth the effort. For Freewheel it was a chance to prove something. For Gaynor, Ron, Gillian, Alison, Anita, Annette, Colleen, Julie, John, Lee, Dave it was, I think, the first time they had read a Shakespeare play, because at school it had been considered too difficult, and so now they leapt at the opportunity to read one, understand it, perform in it and become word perfect. With Angie Lumb's beautiful painted and tie-dyed costumes, Janet Cox's painted cloth and scaffold set (which we could put up in five minutes flat), our show was well received as the reviews indicate. We even attracted business sponsorship from British Telecom. Freewheel, it seemed had arrived! All this could not have happened without the goodwill and effort of so many other people, largely teachers and local students. Richard Penton, of Hull School of Architecture, designed an inspired logo of a freewheeling wheelchair (first worked out on a beer mat in the bar at Spring Street Theatre). Kate Oliver, an Art student, designed the poster and took part. Steve, from the School of Architecture, made an flying set, which we only managed to use once at the University Gulbenkian Theatre (but it was sublime). Mark Jones, a University Drama Student, devised a superb sound tape, helped with transport and listened to my fears, moans and anxieties. We bullied and cajoled actors to stay with us throughout the long haul of rehearsals. It seemed to be in the nature of things that I would think I had got a full cast, and then some one would announce that they couldn't do it because they had found a job, or were going on a course, or were just fed up and so they were leaving. Each week I was prepared for anything.

Soon the group caught on and we were being asked to run workshops in other institutions, such as the Colleges of Further and Higher Education, Hull Students Union and the local PHAB (Physically Handicapped and Able Bodied) club. Inevitably the next blow came when, because of a change in government policy, the MSC-funded Community Care Programme ended and we lost our volunteer carers, drivers and mini-bus overnight! This meant we had to write to local councillors, and nag anyone who might be of any use to us. We didn't hold out much hope, but, somehow, Carol managed to conjure up a bus, escorts and a driver every week, so we carried on.

It was Andrew Dixon, Arts Officer for Humberside County Council, and Sue Roberts, the local Special Needs Arts Officer, who combined their efforts with ours and procured a brand-new, fully adapted, mini-bus for our own use from Hull City Council. So, with Richard Penton's logo and our name Freewheel Theatre Company proudly displayed on the side, we braved yet another year.

Finance was always a headache. For some reason I could raise money for the artistic side, such as production assistant, the set and costume designer fee from the local arts organisations and we were offered advice, free publicity and technical assistance from staff of Spring Street and the Gulbenkian Theatres, but help to strengthen the professional infrastructure of the group, with, for example, a full-time administrator or financial help with maintaining or running the mini-bus, was never forthcoming. Neither did I receive any more paid teaching time. We ran fund-raising events and started to request fees for any workshops we did, but this never matched the time and effort which Debbie, Carol and others increasingly had to give just to keep the show on the road. It soon began to be more of a strain on us all.

Our next production, was *King Ubu*, an adaption of Alfred Jarry's play, *Ubu Roi*. I updated it and set it in Britain at sometime during the 1990s. Pa followed the line of infamous dictators such as Stalin, Hitler and the like. The sheer anarchy of the theme and exuberance of the language appealed to me. We reformed and seemed to keep the majority of the group. Graham left to start a training course, Kate had too much to cope with because of her finals, but Brian managed to work rehearsals round a Restart course. Anita decided that Disabled Sports were more in her line and Mark and Phil, 'the boys', just upped and went. We attracted new people, some who just turned up and asked if we wanted any help, such as Sandra, who everyone fell in love with, and Cheryl, Stuart, Richard, Britta and the two Phils. Quite frankly we did need them, and we didn't hesitate in drawing them in.

*King Ubu* was a departure for Freewheel, because for this production we ventured into song. We employed Ian Heywood, a composer, who commuted from Leeds to write the music. His instructions were to write songs that even I could sing. Quite a tall order. In the end it was his music which was awarded a prize at the All England Theatre Festival, so we had come a long way. This time it was Chris Lee who made our costumes, which were all gold braid and epaulettes. Mark Batty made a set on casters — which worked. Jo Walker designed the poster. Understandably, however, by the time *King Ubu* was up and running the strain of working in an underfunded organisation began to show. By necessity we were too dependent on volunteer help and goodwill, and soon the inevitable emotional blackmail crept in as people were working to full stretch trying to meet production deadlines without properly paid staff. A focus for this frustration was the fact that I had cast Brian and Sandra, both able-bodied and very fine actors, in the lead roles of Ma and Pa Ubu. This seemed to make sense to me ideologically, because, in society the able-bodied take control of the disabled and the play reflected on this. The rest of the group seemed to be happy with this and we discussed it at the time. Brian and Sandra were also excellent in their parts, and again it seemed to me that we were giving parts to people on merit and suitability rather than because they were able-bodied or disabled. In retrospect, I have to admit I had made a mistake and had miscalculated how two able bodied actors in the lead would appear to an audience, and I was criticised for falling back on a safe option by letting the able-bodied have the best parts. I don't think I ever resolved that one.

Finally, I and the group came under fire from full-time adult education staff. One day out of the blue we were informed that we were not doing the 'right' thing. We were told that the members of Freewheel should be empowered to take over the key positions in the group, they and not the able-bodied should be arranging publicity, making costumes, painting the sets and organising the transport. There was a flaw in this position, however, and it proved fatal. As was evident to anyone who knew the group properly, the disabled members didn't want to do any of these things: they wanted to act. I wished they hadn't felt this way, as my life would've been a lot easier, but that was the way it was.

How was it that some people didn't understand that every year we had a democratically elected committee which met once a month which could have changed things at anytime? This was a difficult and stressful time for us all and rumours abounded. It coincided with my decision to return to full-time teaching, but luckily I managed to find Sarah Cheesmond who took over the Artistic Directorship, and carried the group through to Christmas, until she in turn, moved on. However, in spite of all our efforts, the damage had been done, and for the time being perhaps Freewheel was doomed to be beached on the politics of disability! Ironically, this was one idea which Freewheel never seemed to bother about, so long as everyone got a part.

The final word, in this episode of Freewheel's history (and let it not be the finale), should come from one of the members of the group, Gillian Sorfleet. Gillian was in a wheelchair because of Multiple Sclerosis, and she played Ariel and Captain McNure. Long before the 'troubles' commenced she wrote about what she wanted from her weekly drama workshops: 'For as long as I can remember I have wanted to act. But when I became disabled I gave up all hope of ever achieving my ambition, all I had left was my imagination. Then, one day, at Out Patients, another patient who was a member of Freewheel asked me if I was interested in Drama, and that is what changed my life. It opened up a whole new world for me, I made so many new friends and have gone from being alone and bored to being a busy, excited and happily fulfilled person. It means so much to me to be able to give, and that is what we do, not only every time we go on stage, but also in the workshops we do with other groups. Once you are on the stage you are not disabled any more, you are your character and can do all the things your character can do. All you need is an imagination and the belief of your audience. As we are a touring company, we get to travel and see many new places and meet many new people. The accolades one receives make it all so worthwhile and you know you are not useless.'

## FROM A PERSONAL POINT OF VIEW
by Ron Walker

My interest in drama began in the late Sixties when the National Association of Youth Clubs ran courses. These were designed for physically disabled and able-bodied people and normally lasted a week. Each day you would have workshops of music, drama and art etc. To take these subjects there would be professional tutors who had an interest in the work. The able-bodied would not merely come as helpers but, of course, if you needed help it was always there. The main idea of the able-bodied people was that they should not only participate in the residential courses but integrate as much as possible. By doing this it would be hoped that they were breaking down the barriers between the physically handicapped and the able-bodied. I feel also that they were able to stretch the limitations of the disabled and it was interesting to find out what they could do beyond their limitations. After so many of the courses I soon wondered why it should stop there. Even if you are severely disabled and cannot put into practice what you have learnt there is nothing to stop you telling others provided they have the patience to listen.

In Hull we were very fortunate in having the Spring Street Theatre and there they not only performed plays but put on a lot of workshops. I began to attend the improvisation and play-writing workshops.

At first I was quite content to go and listen but the able-bodied who attended had the right attitude and persuaded me to become involved. I became conscious that I wanted to take this further and this opened up a new world for me. I must say that I am very fortunate in having many able-bodied friends who coached me into having a go. I might add that this interest opened yet another new dimension to my life and I truly feel that it is far better than going to day centres where you are only accepted as a disabled person.

There is an organisation called the Winged Fellowship Trust, which has a centre in this part of the country called 'Skylarks' in Nottingham. I happened to find out that they run a number of courses during the off peak season, one being a drama fortnight. I applied and it was most interesting. We not only performed a play but during the fourteen-day course we actually wrote it. But I never expected that one day we should see a disabled drama group would be started up in Hull.

The Hull Community Care Team soon found out there were a number of disabled people of the same mind, and in 1985, under the guidance of Pam Dellar, an eight week drama workshop started. The interest soon grew when she realised that there were quite a lot of physically disabled people who have much potential and want to be stretched beyond their limitations. She encouraged us to embark on a production, *Variations on a Theme of Oz*, and then another based on Voltaire's *Candide* in which I played Dr. Pangloss. We devised the scenes at rehearsal and then wrote them up. In the play our Candide was unemployed, that was why he had to go out and seek his fortune. During our rehearsals Jenny Foreman used to come in and give instructions in mask making. She became so interested in the group that when Pam retired she applied for the job as Artistic Director. It was then that we changed our name to Freewheel Theatre Co. Jenny proved to be so enthusiastic that she very soon surprised us with her suggestion that she would like to produce Shakespeare's *The Tempest*. She did however recognise that we would not be able to portray it in its entirety but she was convinced that the main story was interesting and something we could get our teeth into. Eight months of really hard work from Jenny and lots of concentration and co-operation from us proved worthwhile when we finally staged part of it in the local heats of the All England Drama Festival, where we were commended. We did the whole adaption at the Spring Street Theatre and at the Gulbenkian Theatre, Hull University, all of which were well attended much to our delight.

Our next production was *King Ubu* by Alfred Jarry and we took both productions over to Derbyshire. We also participated in integrated open access workshops in the community and continued the weekly workshop at Fredrick Homes School which offered young disabled students access to the performing arts. Jenny was very aware that disabled people can, if given the right opportunities and encouragement, achieve much more than many folk give us credit for.

We gained a lot of help from Hull Community Care Team and many volunteers who made the costumes and scenery.

In September, 1988, through the generosity of Humberside County Council we obtained a new mini-bus to take wheelchairs. This was not only to get us to rehearsals but to various venues to perform our plays. It was a nice change not to have to rely on other organisations for our transport.

It was great how we brought able-bodied young people into the company. Personally I would not have been interested if it had just involved the physically handicapped. If you have young able-bodied people in the group, as we did, you are going another step forward. The able-bodied can encourage you to do even more things than you thought possible. This is why I believe in the PHAB philosophy.

When you think about it we really did achieve quite a lot in those four years with P.R.A.T.S. and Freewheel, not only with our plays but taking them to the All England Theatre Festival and competing alongside other drama companies. For myself, I enjoyed what I did in P.R.A.T.S. and Freewheel and surely that's the main thing.

I believe that our company was unique in many ways; it certainly showed that disabled people are capable of doing a lot more than the general public presume. Also, as an integrated company, it showed disabled people can work alongside able-bodied people providing that the management structures are correct. It would be a great shame if all our hard work and past commitment came to nothing.

This is why I'm delighted to say that the foundations for a new Integrated Theatre Company have been laid through the integrated Drama Course. This course was organised by 'Artlink' at Arts International College, Bubwith, North Yorkshire, which I was pleased to attend. During our stay, it became quite clear that there is a positive need for an Integrated Theatre Company and a core group of committed people have been identified through the course.

*In September, 1992, over two years since its last production,* Freewheel
Theatre Company *is still without the professional infrastructure it needs to
become fully operational again.* Editor

*Meta van Delden Paterson shows Sam the Sailor to a group of Cottingham children, 1966.*

*The Civic Society's winning float in the Lord Mayor's Parade, 1972, with the Theatre for Children and Hull Truck. Centre, with the long sword, Donald Campbell, Right of him is Mike Bradwell and next to him John Lee. Centre back is Alen Davis.*

(*Photograph by courtesy of the* Hull Daily Mail)

*Costume designs by John Munday for*
The Owl and the Pussycat Went to See
*by David Woods. Sets by Alan Davis.*

Roland Gift as the highjacker in the Community Theatre Workshop's version of Voltaire's Candide, 1977.

A Farthing For Public Opinion, 1974 — an early community play — sets designed by Alan Davis. The statue is King Billy in Hull Market Place.

The Sea by Edward Bond, 1977. Hull Art College Theatre Group. '. . . please don't try to hustle me into a purchase . . .'

The Marat/Sade, 1974. Hull Art College Theatre Group. '. . . we want our revolution NOW!'

(Photograph by courtesy of Alan Davis)

*Poster by Sarah Nash, 1981, for Outreach Community Arts.*

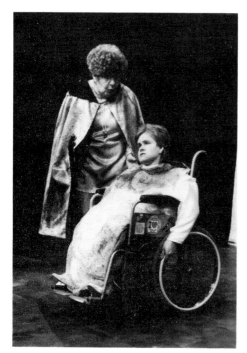

*Freewheel Theatre Company in their version of* The Tempest. '. . . *art to enchant* . . .'

CHAPTER FIVE

# WOMEN'S THEATRE IN HULL 1978-1988
by Jane Thomas

'We make theatre out of our lives, our dreams our feelings, our fantasies. We make theatre by letting out the different parts of us that we have pushed inside all our lives...Making theatre out of these private parts of ourselves is one way we are trying every day to take our own experiences seriously, to accept our feelings as valid and real.'

During the 1970s committed theatre found a growing outlet in traditionally non-theatre venues: town halls, community and day centres, clubs and student union meeting rooms, and on the street. This gradual move outside the professional theatre system was often deliberate and frequently unavoidable. Committed theatre challenged the status quo with its controversial political content and its belief that the theatrical experience itself should be made available to a broader section of the community. This meant locating new audiences and also questioning the assumption that serious theatre, in all its aspects, necessarily belonged to trained professionals. Committed theatre began to concern itself with new issues in addition to political propaganda including self-expression and the value of authentic, lived experience. These issues combined to produce their maximum impact in the form of anti-prop, street theatre and community theatre. The 1970s also saw the growth, spread and consolidation of the Women's Movement in the United States and Britain and its gradual infiltration into the areas of class and radical as well as gender oppression. On the 20 November, 1970, the twentieth Miss World Contest, held in the Royal Albert Hall, London was disrupted by a group of women protesting against the sexual objectification of women in beauty contests. The following year the protest, this time contained by security forces outside the Albert Hall, was led by The Women's Street Theatre Group who dramatised their objections by parading round the building dressed in dark clothes with flashing lights attached to their nipples and crotches. Blatant but indisputably to the point! Street theatre and sexual politics became close companions from that day on.

On Thursday, 17 May, 1978, Hull Women's Collective Theatre Group, in association with the Community Theatre Workshop and ably supported directed and encouraged by Pamela Dellar staged an improvised play at the then Humberside Theatre called *A Woman Alone,* followed by a short, punchy feminist review originally devised to provide a second half to the evening. The review contained sketches and songs, some original and some borrowed from the repertoire of a Women's Collective in London. They were grouped under three headings: Women and Education, dealing with gender-stereotyping of school girls and featuring Dennis the Menace, and Peggy Seagar's Song *I Wanna Be an Engineer;* Women and Work, which focused on women's unpaid work in the home and incorporated a rewrite of the Cinderella story; and Women and Mental Health which centred on the high incidence of nervous breakdowns and clinical depression among women. High points of the review included a sketch by Beryl Dellar, *Brave New World,* in which a housewife relieves her suicidal depression by shooting a persistent door-to-door salesman, and *Beat the Doctor,* a game show in which two housewives endeavour to complete the day's domestic chores and remain sane. The Grand Finale was the song that was to provide the group with the name it retained for the next four years:

*We're Shameless Hussies and we don't give a damn*
*We're loud and raucous and we're fighting for our rights*
*For our sex, for our fun,*
*And we're strong, and we're strong.*
*Men call us names to be nasty and crude*
*Like Lesbian, man-hater, bitch and prostitute*
*What a laugh! Ha, ha, ha!*
*'Cos a half of it's true.*
*This docile fragile image of our sex must die, must die.*
*From centuries of silence we are screaming into action.*
*We're Shameless Hussies and we curse and we swear*
*We'll be free, beware to those who disagree.*
*Come and fight, come and sing.*
*And we'll win, and we'll win.*

The play was received with supportive, considered applause: the review was appreciative foot-stamping and whistling. Humberside's first Community Women's Theatre Group was born.

From May, 1979, to February, 1980, Hull Women's Collective Theatre Group recruited new enthusiastic members, including myself, and performed various reviews and cabaret shows in venues ranging from the Humberside Theatre and Hull College to Fountain Road Community Centre. We also provided polemical entertainment at the official opening of Hull Women's Centre on Middleton Street. New and original sketches and songs were devised to supplement old favourites and we adopted an official 'costume' of black 'T'-shirts and black trousers. We met once a week at the drama studio on the Cottingham Road site of what is now Humberside University, for workshops in voice production, drama games, and to read, refine and rehearse the sketches we had written at home.

In our quest for new audiences we descended on an unwary bingo session at Fountain Road Community Centre one evening, encouraged by reports that the participants were predominantly female. The men, it transpired, were exhibiting their cacti in an adjacent room. The organiser encouraged the bingo players, many of them middle-aged and elderly women, to stay on after the end of the session as 'some young ladies' had come to entertain them. Capitalising on this, one of our musical members played *If You Were The Only Girl in The World* in the interval and the rest of us led the group in a sing-song of some of their favourite old tunes. After 20 minutes our audience was nicely warmed up and looking forward to more of the same later on. One or two of the cacti growers had drifted in to join us between judgings. When the second half of the bingo session ended we closed the exit doors, dimmed the lights and burst onto the stage with the first verse of *The Woman's Hokey-Cokey* — 'You put the nappies in, the nappies out, in out, in out, you shake them all about...' Much of the song was lost amid the shocked and disgruntled scrape of chairs and rattling of exit doors. However, we concluded it with a good three-quarters of the original audience still doggedly in their seats. As the review progressed we got the distinct impression that some of them were actually beginning to enjoy themselves as sniggers and titters grew into uninhibited laughter and applause, occasionally punctured by the appearance of a bemused cactus grower. Half way through the Cinderella sketch one lady was heard to mutter 'That's all we are — bloody slaves', at which point her long suffering male companion snorted, 'Right, that's enough of that. You're coming home.' The show ended with a spontaneous conga across the stage and round the hall led by ourselves with most of the audience clinging on behind.

Hull Women's Collective Theatre Group went through a number of changes as founder members — Chris Walker, Cathy Welsh and Caroline Goddard — finished their college courses and went to London in search of employment. Under our new name, and with many new members we began to analyse our politics and our potential. We made a conscious decision to exclude men from the group and to perform work which was by and about women. All women were welcome to join us regardless of their skills or experience. We favoured collective scripting and group direction over hierarchy and authoritarian control, and tried to ensure that no member of the group was compromised or disturbed by any of the sketches or their implications. Worries and disagreements were tackled in rehearsal or, failing that, in the main bar of the Polar Bear at the end of the meeting. We tried to incorporate the many different and contradictory manifestations of 'Feminism' as well as the occasional 'I'm not a feminist but...'

Our decision to write a short play protesting against John Corrie's proposed amendment to the 1967 Abortion Act led to a lot of anguish, dissension and compromise but in February, 1980, Shamless Hussies produced *You Can't Win* in an attempt to explore the implications of Corrie's Bill. *You Can't Win* was performed at Humberside College of Art and we closed the evening with a discussion prefaced by a 'hot-spot' session in which each of us was interrogated in character by members of the audience.

Shortly after this our rehearsal space in Cottingham Road was damaged in a fire (nothing to do with Shameless Hussies I hasten to add) and we moved under the umbrella of Outreach Community Arts which had been recently established in Northumberland Avenue. Along with other community theatre groups we benefited from Outreach's excellent facilities and the skills of of its talented and committed staff who designed and painted flats, shifted props, scenery and personnel and applied for funding on our behalf.

The 1970s had witnesses the emergence of Feminist Drama as a distinct genre designed to challenge the paucity of positive and major female roles. At the same time feminist presses such as Virago were republishing works by forgotten or disregarded women writers, and re-introducing classic texts by women such as Charlotte Perkins Gilman's *The Yellow Wallpaper* — a short but compelling account of a nervous breakdown by a 19th-century middle-class American woman. The narrator, also named Charlotte, describes her slow deterioration under Dr. S. Weir Mitchell's renowned 'Rest Cure' prescribed as an antidote to post-natal depression brought on by 'inappropriate ambition'. The 'Cure', comprising weeks of mental and physical inactivity in a darkened room, seems to have deranged more women than it helped, as is the case with the fictional Charlotte. An intelligent, lively authoress forbidden the distractions of human companionship and pen and paper, she becomes obsessed with the hideous yellow wallpaper in the locked bedroom in which she was kept, and imagines that she sees a woman caught up in the tendrils and coils of the pattern. Gradually she comes to identify with the trapped woman, with tragic consequences. One or two of us had read the book and, at Pam Dellar's instigation, I adapted it for the stage. The first draft was much amended and improved by the group. On 21 June, 1980, the Shameless Hussies presented *The Yellow Wallpaper* to a packed house at the Humberside Theatre. Our adaption kept very close to the original novel using voice overs and special lighting effects to convey the deterioration and mental trauma of Charlotte, a single, lonely figure in a nightmare room.

Our membership grew significantly as a direct result of this production but we were forced to confront the fact that none of us was skilled in the techniques of lighting and sound and we were having to rely on male technicians to produce the show. Some of them were sympathetic, some of them were not. So, while interested members of the group tackled the intricacies of fresnels and gobos, the rest of us turned increasingly to street theatre and reviews. Props were kept to the minimum — a guitar, half a dozen kazoos and a banner — and for special performances indoors we invested in a glorious purple, silver and green glitter curtain. New songs and sketches were added to the repetoire which reflected our increasing anger at the siting of missiles on British bases, the inadequacies of the equal pay act, the conditions for working women especially in the realms of childcare and the sheer difficulties of functioning as women in our male-dominated society. *Argon Calling* featured a saleswomen extolling the merits of the 'utility bag' full of essential little items for today's woman on the street, including a brick, sharp stilettos and a mousetrap — 'mustn't forget the flashers must we?' *My Old Ma*... was a parody of *My Old Man's a Dustman:* each verse described the available female careers, including cleaner, office worker and mother, with a blank space for the audience to fill in the final missing word. *The Contraceptive Song* was, as its title suggests, a humorous excursion through the available methods of birth control with a refrain demanding a safer, more convenient alternative (someone informed me Ben Elton has recently done a sketch along similar lines). *Living Man* was an 'affectionate' alternative version of Cliff Richard's famous hit.

Other parodies included *Stand on Your Man*, and *Women are a Girl's Best Friend*. We also wrote a new verse to Leon Rosselson's *Don't Get Married, Girls* to celebrate the Royal Wedding. I suppose looking back on it it was hardly surprising that our applications for funding fell on stony ground. Our material was simple and deliberately shocking and aimed at breaking the taboos concerning what was acceptable behaviour for women and we issued direct challenges to our audiences — especially the male members. Our lyrics were crude, our imagery was extravagant and exaggerated and our techniques were far from polished but we were in big demand. We played at Hull University Union for a Women's Voice Day-school which discussed such issues as 'Violence Against Women', 'A Woman's Right to Work', and 'Contraception'.

We were in cabaret downstairs at the Wellington Club; at a Women's Aid Conference in Leeds; and at York Arts Centre. We also did a spot of street theatre outside the City Hall and on Whitefriargate, much to the bemusement of the local bobby who turned up with his walkie talkie so that the officers back at the station could hear us and advise him accordingly. Needless to say we were gently 'moved on'. We played at 'Women-only' Discos at the Wellington Club, The Bull, and Spring Bank Community Centre. All this happened in the first six months of 1981 and many of us had full-time jobs, college and university work to do and families to look after.

Our most controversial performance was our *Late Night Cabaret* on the opening night of the National Student Drama Festival which in 1981 was held in Hull. Our audience was composed of an explosive mix of army Cadets and Rugby Club members who had come for the bar extension, and genuinely interested Festival goers including feminists and regular Hussy fans. The more we were heckled the more aggressively we performed and it became harder and harder for anyone who wanted to hear us. By the end of the show fights were breaking out in the audience, which was divided between heckling us and abusing one another. We escaped shocked and exhilarated but in one piece. Our show provoked a storm of controversy in *Noises Off* — the review magazine specially published by the festival — and the reverberations were felt throughout the whole week

Even the reviewer of Victoria Wood's one-woman show in the Middleton Hall couldn't resist a sideways swipe at the Shameless Hussies, who were also mentioned in the final assessment of events.

We ended the year with a 1980s rewrite of the Nativity story in which the part of the Angel Gabriel was played by a doctor confirming the results of a pregnancy test and Baby Jesus was nearly taken away from his mother because of the insanitary conditions in which he was born. The Christmas show was performed at various community venues including a Mother's Group on Bransholme.

May, 1982, had been chosen for a nationwide celebration of women in the Arts and Entertainment. A week of events was planned at Humberside Theatre including films, an exhibition of paintings and sculpture, poetry readings and the Shameless Hussies in *Winifred: A Dramatic Portrait of the Life and Times of Winifred Holtby*. In a deliberate change of direction we took up a suggestion that had originally been made by Pam's husband, Harold Dellar, and began to concern ourselves with the life and writings of Hull's most famous woman novelist and political journalist. Using material from her works, letters and biographical material, and Vera Brittain's *Testament of Friendship*, we co-scripted a tribute to Winifred consisting of scenes from her friendship with Vera Brittain interspersed with dramatised sections of her novels. The production was directed by Pam and entirely stage managed by members of the group and we even bought our own Front-of-House Organiser. The response to the play was very favourable.

Much of 1982 was taken up with *Winifred* and recovering from the enormous task of writing and performing the play. We closed with another Christmas show aimed at the domestic and commercial pressures of the festive season which we performed, tired and under-rehearsed, at Spring Bank Community Centre.

In April and May of 1983 we entered on our most ambitious project — an East Riding Tour of *Winifred*. We opened the tour at Humberside Theatre with roughly the same script and cast and then went on to evening performances in schools in Cottingham, Withernsea and Hornsea. Fatigue, staleness and poor audiences rather dented our enthusiasm. The Shameless Hussies had come a long way from our early 'relax and have fun' days — probably as far as we could go under the circumstances. The Shameless Hussies disbanded shortly after their final performance of *Winifred* at Hornsea School on 21 May 1983.

Earlier in the year Hull Truck Theatre Company had taken over the distressed Humberside Theatre, renamed it Spring Street Theatre and rejuvenated it with a massive injection of grant aid and an exciting programme of drama, dance and cabaret as well as newly commissioned plays for Hull Truck from their recently appointed Artistic Director, John Godber. In September I was appointed Community Theatre Director with a brief to consolidate and extend the links between the community, Hull Truck and other professional companies performing at the theatre. I immediately set about forging new links with schools and community centres, and established a programme of workshops led by visiting professional companies, as well as regular in-house sessions covering play-writing, poetry, fiction and women's theatre.

In the course of my private research I discovered that Hull's extremely active Women's Suffrage Society was the first outside London to receive the Annual Convention of the National Union of Women's Suffrage Societies on October 20, 1905. Gathering together a team of willing researchers I began to find out as much as I could about the Hull Society from old newspaper reports of the time housed in the Central Library. An advertisement in the *Hull Star* resulted in a number of letters and before long I had enough material for a play on the subject. *The Hull Suffragettes* was a combination of documentary and oral history interspersed with three plays written by the Actresses Franchise League in the early part of the century to publicise the cause of Women's suffrage. Edwardian parlour music was provided in the interval and the audience was invited to dress up in period costume. The play opened at Spring Street on 9 July, 1984, and ran for two nights. At that time Hull Truck was lucky to have the excellent services of their Publicity Officer, Phillippa Johnston, who contacted the YTV *Calendar* programme. There couldn't have been much happening in Humberside and Lincolnshire that day because much to our surprise a full camera crew complete with interviewer turned up to our dress rehearsal. The theatre was packed on both nights. We had drafted in some of the male members of Hull Truck's staff to play the parts of policemen, and a very compliant John Godber gave a convincing performance as an anti-suffrage speaker. The audience entered into the proceedings with great gusto, cheering, booing and clapping in all the right places.

During the re-enactment of the arrest of Laetitia Marsh — the Yorkshire Organiser of the Women's Social and Political Union, one elderly lady got completely carried away and started to set about the 'policeman" leaving him with what could have been a rather serious injury!

*The Hull Suffragettes* returned to Spring Street Theatre by popular request for two more nights in October of the same year.

From this time on Spring Street Women's Theatre Workshop went from strength to strength recruiting members from a variety of backgrounds — students, teachers fifth formers, a telephonist, a D.H.S.S. clerk and a number of unemployed women. Many of us were active feminists — radical, liberal and lesbian. Others refused to be drawn on political issues but liked the atmosphere of the group. Some of us had acted before but many were totally inexperienced. Our ages ranged from 16 to 40-something and we were united by our love of theatre and the fact that we enjoyed the company of other women. In addition to those who wanted to act there were others who were solely interested in the technical side of making theatre.

The group decided that it wanted to tackle the complexities of a scripted play — preferably written by a women and with a large number of female parts. Among the many professional women's theatre groups who played at the Humberside Theatre and, later, Spring Street Theatre was Monstrous Regiment who had premiered *Vinegar Tom* by Caryl Churchill there in 1979. Joint Stock Theatre Group performed Churchill's *Cloud Nine* in the same year and both productions had made a deep impression on those of us who had watched them so we decided to look more closely at Churchill's work. *Top Girls* was pronounced ideal.

Separating each character, rather than doubling up as the script suggested, meant that there was a maximum of 16 parts available. The play was complex and demanding for both the acting and production teams but we all liked it. However, some members of the group were concerned that the play appeared to present women in a negative light in that it had no solution to the dilemma of chosing between domestic fulfilment and a satisfying career.

The play prompted a number of animated and intense discussions in the bar of Spring Street Theatre during which we got to know ourselves and each other better. We also came up with a new name — Company of Women — which seemed to sum up in a neat pun what we enjoyed most about the group. It also gave us an interesting acronym!.

The play was presented at Spring Street Theatre for three nights from 30 May to 1 June and was co-directed by myself and fellow member Fiona Welburn who later went on to train at Bretton Hall College. She is now a professional actress and recently appeared at Spring Street Theatre as a member of the cast of Remould Theatre Company's play *Street Beat*. Despite one or two minor hitches we were very proud of this production and in particular of our three-woman stage management team who were required to strike a three-course banquet for seven people, complete with wine and coffee, in less than three minutes. The reviews were favourable too.

1985 was the 50th anniversary of the death of Winifred Holtby and Hull City Council had decided to honour her in that year's Hull Festival. The festival featured a revival of the *Dramatic Portrait of the Life and Work of Winifred Holtby'*, written and re-named simply *Winifred*.

Of the original Shameless Hussies cast only myself, Gill Holtby and Pam Dellar, who was to direct the revised play, were available. I was very pleased to play the part of Winifred to Jenny Foreman's Vera. Other parts were taken by women from the community, including the writer Audrey Dunne and Gillian Holtby, who is directly related to Winifred, along with members of Splash Theatre Company, who also stage-managed the production. Jenny, Pam and myself did a lot of research in order to re-create as accurate a picture of Winifred and Vera as possible. We were greatly assisted by the fact that a revival in interest in women writers had led to the reprinting of much of Winifred and Vera's work, mostly by Virago Press.

It was almost a year before Company of Women trod the boards again. The Women's Theatre Workshop had continued to meet each week and, as the group began to consolidate, we decided that it was time to concentrate on another project. Each week members brought along books by women that they had enjoyed reading and the group assessed their suitability for adaption and possible presentation. Sharon Lill, an active member of Company of Women, had photocopied some dialogue from a novel by the North East writer Pat Barker called *Blow Your House Down*. She had also adapted some scenes from the book which she bought along to a meeting. We read the dialogue and were unanimous in our enthusiasm.

The book provoked a lot of soul-searching and dispute among the members of the group as each of us was forced to analyse and re-assess our opinions on everything from single parents to prostitution and from the low-level banter and abuse we received on the streets to the fear we experienced going out at night unaccompanied. Some women left the group for personal reasons. One or two felt that our basic ignorance of the realities of prostitution disqualifies us from presenting it on stage. Others were unable to cope with the explicit nature of the subject matter of the book. After the dust had settled I went away and endeavoured to produce a play based on the novel. I returned after the Christmas break with a rough script entitled *The Chicken Factory*. It was polished and refined by the rest of the group and before long we began work on what was to be the most exciting and challenging theatre project I had ever been involved in. Most of the parts were relatively easy to assign but the main character, Jean, defeated us for a while. Jean's part was discouragingly long and demanding. The women who played her had to have a commanding stage presence and a strong Newcastle accent.

In the course of my duties at Spring Street I had to attend a Lincolnshire and Humberside Arts Visual Arts Forum Meeting at the Usher Gallery in Lincoln. I travelled over with Louise West (now Karlsen), the Senior Keeper of the Ferens Art Gallery. On the way back we discussed various matters including her involvement in the Women's Peace Movement and the Folk scene, and mine in Women's Theatre. As I was listening to her warm, Geordie tones I was suddenly struck by an idea and asked how she would feel about joining Company of Women. With careful flattery, and a few white lies I persuaded her to audition for the part of Jean and gave her one of Jean's shorter speeches. She was ideal. When we had encouraged her to commit herself we came clean. Jean was, in fact, the most important character in the play and her part consisted of several intense and lengthy monologues.

With *The Chicken Factory* we finally realised our ambition to mount a production using an all-female production team as well as an all-female cast. Carol Vieira, who later left Hull to pursue a professional acting career, managed the technical side with a little help from Hull Truck's Lighting Designer, Eamonn Hunt. The sound tape was mixed by Soo Ostler who ran her own film-making business and now works for Yorkshire Arts Association, and the play was directed by myself. Soo and I found that we had a lot in common beside our mutual interest in feminism and theatre. We were both six months pregnant.

Motivated by a genuine belief in the play, tinged with a touch of naughtiness, we entered the first act of *The Chicken Factory* for the 'All England Theatre Festival' which was scheduled to take place at Spring Street that Easter. Not only was the subject matter of the play decidedly controversial, its language was extremely likely to cause offence. Needless to say, we didn't win, although the adjudicator commended our portrayal of the 'ladies of the night'!

*The Chicken Factory* ran for three nights at Spring Street Theatre. Thanks to Philippa's provocative press release we received a good deal of advance publicity in the local press which ran articles with titles like 'TERROR ON THE STREETS AT NIGHT'. The play sold out on each of the three nights and I remember feeling extremely moved when the audience broke out into spontaneous applause at the end of one of Louise's powerful monologues. I can also remember those few minutes of thoughtful silence between the ending of the play and the audience's appreciative response.

The final night party was a triumphant occasion tinged with sadness for me as it marked the end of my involvement with women's theatre in Hull. Shortly after the birth of my first daughter I moved from full-time to part-time employment at Spring Street Theatre. Company of Women continued to produce cabaret shows with the support of my co-worker Sue Caudle who is also a member of the group. Their shows brought back lots of memories of the early days of their 'mother' group the Shameless Hussies.

I eventually left Spring Street Theatre to take up a part-time appointment at Hull University, and Hull Truck implemented a new policy with regard to Community Theatre which effectively discouraged amateur theatre groups from meeting and rehearsing there. At the time of writing this piece I am not aware of the existence of any Women's Theatre Groups in Hull.

There is still plenty to protest about as far as the position of women is concerned. However, cuts in Arts funding have jeopardised the existence of professional theatre companies and Arts Centres. Community and amateur theatre rarely pays for itself, in the economic sense of the term, and is so often the first thing to go when resources are scarce. Its value in personal terms, however, is inestimable which is why over 100 women from different backgrounds and age ranges found fulfilment and enjoyment in addition to developing their skills and confidence in the course of their involvement with a decade of women's theatre in Hull.

# CHAPTER SIX

# THE STORY OF THE NORTHERN THEATRE COMPANY

### by Richard Green

Amy Johnson is a popular heroine in Hull and her reputation as a woman flyer has brought fame to the City but she would have been surprised to know that she was inspirational in founding a theatre company.

In 1975 I decided to write a musical about her life. Ian Butler wrote the score, I wrote the libretto and directed the show and Bryan Williams designed all aspects of the production. We put it on at the New Theatre, Hull, and called ourselves the Northern Theatre Company. We had a mixed professional and amateur cast and Doreen Kaye travelled from her home near Scarborough to rehearse the part of Amy which she played with great vitality and panache.

Financially it was not easy to launch the show but luckily a member of a well-known Hull family stepped in as a guarantor. The show was a great hit and played to packed houses in Hull and in Bridlington. A number of London agents expressed an interest in it and in fact Ray Cooney himself nearly bought it but after protracted negotiations chose to do a short-lived musical based on *The Merchant of Venice* instead. The reason he gave for deciding not to do it was that Andrew Lloyd Webber and Alan Ayckbourn had just put on the musical *Jeeves*, which flopped, and Cooney didn't feel like risking another 20s/30s type show so soon. We revived *Amy* again at the request of the City Council in 1982, as part of the Hull Festival that year.

I had been writing plays and musicals for quite a while before *Amy* but could not find a management to put them on. So I decided the only way to get them seen was to put them on myself and this was the *raison d'être* for the Northern Theatre Company in its early days.

The next production was *Piaf* which we staged as a small scale musical at the Library Theatre. In many ways I enjoyed it more than *Amy*. I felt that it would be impossible to do justice to Piaf's amazing voice so she did not sing on stage at all. As it turned out it was just as well for I found an actress who was able to play the diminutive waif-like woman to perfection but lacked a strong singing voice. This was Liz Meech who is now well-known

as a broadcaster on Radio Humberside. I sent the script of *Piaf* to the Royal
Shakespeare Theatre Company but they wrote back to say that they didn't
do musicals. Six months later they announced they would be putting on a
musical play by Jane Lapotoire. It was about Piaf!

I went on to co-write the life story if Marie Lloyd with Norman Parker.
Maggie North made an earthy and dynamic Marie. Then I wrote *Dietrich,
Novello,* and *Over My Shoulder,* which was, of course, based on the life of
Jessie Mathews. I seemed to have hit the mood of the time as I discovered
when I attempted to interest West End managements in them. Other more
well-known writers were also writing their own versions on the same
subjects!.

Strong drama was also part of our company policy and I directed *I
Claudius, Beckett* and John Whiting's *The Devils.* I even attempted a not
very successful production of Oscar Wilde's *Salome* which we put on at the
New Theatre. I tried to present it in Artaudian style but the text didn't seem
to lend itself to this interpretation or at least I couldn't find the right way to
treat it, unlike Lyndsay Kemp who created a memorable version in
London, 1977. At the same time we presented popular musicals like
*Cabaret, Sweet Charity, The King and I* and *South Pacific,* always using
mixed amateur and professional casts and drawing on Hull's considerable
strength in amateur operatic performers.

Most of the shows did well at the box office but *Annie,* our most popular
show of all time, which had filled the New Theatre's 1,100 seats for a
fortnight, was financially a dismal failure. We'd struck a very bad deal over
ticket sales with the manager of the New Theatre and their gain was our loss.
It nearly caused the collapse of the company.

Some shows brought with them attendant problems. For instance, when
we were doing the shows about famous stars I got some strange letters
complaining that I was taking advantage of their past popularity. *Over My
Shoulder* brought threats of legal action from Evelyn Laye, who married
Jessie Mathews' former husband, Sonnie Hale, after a rather messy divorce
case. She nearly stopped us staging it, but our solicitor, rightly as it turned
out, advised us to go ahead. But the solicitor's fees cost us money and we
made a loss on the show; in fact we were getting deeply into debt. I was
teaching at Sidmouth Street Junior School during the day and also had to
take on external productions for operatic societies to support the finances of
the Northern Theatre Company.

One play I wrote in 1977 was about Rudolf Hess. I was fascinated by the
isolation of this man and the mystery surrounding his long years imprisoned
in Spandau. I spent many hours researching his life and seeking the
motivation for his flight to Britain during the war. The mystery, of course,
remains unsolved. We staged the play at the Library Theatre in a
production designed by Bryan Williams who has designed all the Northern
Theatre Company's shows. His posters incorporated the swastika in the

design and this created local opposition to the play. Then one day to my surprise I received a letter from a neo-Nazi party couched in threatening terms. Later there was a phone call from a lady with a heavy European accent. She said she was a relative of Hess. She and her family were worried that we were trying to do Hess down. Leave us alone, she continued, the family had suffered enough already. In reply, I explained that my real concern was with the humanity of the man and the despair of his present situation.

By now, working with such large numbers of people was causing a problem over finding rehearsal rooms and we also needed space to store Bryan's sets and our props and costumes which up to now had been kept in my mother's spare bedroom in her house in Hotham Road. We were lucky. A sponsor offered to invest in property in Cottingham which we could then use for the Northern Theatre Company. It was an ex-TV-dealer's shop which had the advantage of workshops at the rear. It was here that we founded the Northern Theatre Company School of the Performing Arts as a means of providing firm financial backing for the company.

So the work of the company continued. We even toured our productions. *A Little Of What You Fancy* played for a week at the Leeds City Varieties Theatre, *Over My Shoulder* went to the Floral Hall, Scarborough, and *Sweet Charity* played a week at the Theatre Royal, Lincoln. We have also taken part in street theatre, performed at garden fêtes and the Edwardian Sunday and taken shows to stately homes: Sledmere House, Burton Constable Hall and Carlton Towers.

In 1983 Hull City Council commissioned the company to write an original musical based on the life of William Wilberforce for Hull Festival. Norman Parker and I wrote the show and Laurence Rugg wrote the music.

As I researched I became increasingly disillusioned when I discovered that Wilberforce was not quite the hero that people would have him to be. To me it seemed that his efforts to free the slaves had more to do with his desire to save white souls than his concern for black people. I played Wilberforce and during the week of performances was very unwell with a bad attack of diahorrea. Odd, really, because Wilberforce suffered from exactly the opposite problem. I didn't know whether to be pleased when people told me I looked exactly like him. YTV filmed me riding in a horse-drawn carriage and dismounting in the High Street outside Wilberforce House.

Hull is twinned with Sierra Leone and some of their officials came over for the celebrations. I recall that our whole cast was later entertained by them at a reception in the Guildhall.

But now we were beginning to feel the need for our own theatre. The New Theatre was too large for some shows and Spring Street Theatre had reduced its availability for local outside productions. Our Northern Theatre Company School too was flourishing, undoubtedly influenced by the success of the American TV, show *Fame*, but also providing something for young people that had been up to then lacking in the City. It was around this time too that the City Council started to provide us with an annual grant of £2,000 which helped our running costs.

We started looking at property and finally Larards, the estate agents, came up with one that seemed suitable. It was the disused City Temple at the corner of Madeley Street and Hessle Road and it was up for sale with the old school building next to it. Hessle Road is regarded with affection by many people in Hull for it is where the fishing community used to live. For a time it went into decay and disuse when many residents were moved to Bransholme, a large outer estate, but new Council policies were being adopted and funds were becoming available to help regenerate life in this inner area of the City. To put a theatre and school of performing arts there seemed almost foolhardy but there was a precedent in the early 1950s when Stella Sizer Simpson ran her Janus Theatre in the very next street to our proposed theatre. The building was in a very poor state but the price was low. We bought it for around £16,000.

We envisaged the lower part of the redundant church as being used for a scenic workshop and store, adding a floor at balcony level to accommodate the Studio Theatre. The school building, of course, would house the School of Performing Arts. We applied to the City Council for a grant but didn't get one. We went ahead anyway. Bryan took on the main responsibility for planning and design and we worked day and night to convert the building and decorate it. Bryan was also lecturing part-time at the College of Art and I was teaching all day so it wasn't easy. Then the money ran out.

We found that we couldn't afford to heat and maintain both church and school and so eventually decided to move everything into the school. But having set out to establish a theatre we were still going to do it.

Bryan drew up plans to turn the largest room into a little theatre seating 60 people. There was no way we could get rid of a great iron pillar in the middle of it so we decided it would have to stay and Bryan has ever since devised sets which incorporate the pillar as part of the scenery. It has been fireplaces, trees, chimneys, street corners, bus stops, balconies, a street light and — a pillar!

Because of fire restrictions we have had to keep all dressing rooms and the bar on the ground floor — only then could we obtain a proper theatre licence. We called our theatre Studio 2.

But no sooner had the theatre opened than the City Council announced a new policy decision: arts revenue support was to be limited to only a few clients and we were not amongst them. By then we were seriously in debt. The bank was threatening to foreclose. In desperation I rang Councillor Pat Doyle, the leader of the City Council. He had always shown a sympathetic interest in our work. To cut a long story short, he arranged a meeting with the City Council Finance Committee. They agreed to take on the mortgage.

We then paid interest to them and not the bank and for the next few years received project funding of £1,500. This was on condition that we had a management committee, which now takes on much of the burden of financial management. A social committee also helps with fund raising. Over the years we have managed to maintain the building but it is still not repaired and there is a serious fault in the wing.

It took some time to persuade our audience to travel at night into the Hessle Road area, for its reputation as a hard-drinking place still remained, until people gradually realised that it was just under the flyover of the new by-pass and was really easy to find. The school helped of course and we are now assisted by part-time staff who prepare students for external exams: Sadie Ellerby, Paul Shepherdson, Richard Vergette and Katie Lutkin. Dance training was given by Margaret Watson and now by Julie Burton. We try to make opportunities for the pupils to play in other venues to give them the experience of working on larger stages, and recently they did *The Wizard of Oz* at the Library Theatre and *Bugsy Malone* at the New Theatre (1989). They also appear with visiting companies at the New Theatre and from time to time get paid work with B.B.C. and Independent Television. Of course I should make it clear that it is not a full-time stage school. The pupils come to us after school and at weekends and in holiday time. In the summer holiday we run a summer school where children come from all over to take part in a week's project in dance and drama which culminates in performances in Studio 2. It's hard work but they love it. Then each term also sees a review-style entertainment based on the work of musical theatre classics.

Today the Studio Theatre provides space for our own company. Recent productions have included Berkoff's *Metamorphosis, Cat on a Hot Tin Roof, After the Fall* and *All My Sons*. It is also a venue for many local amateur dramatic societies. We charge them a small fee and provide free publicity and front of house and box office. There are also productions by the Northern Theatre Company Youth Theatre.

Between October and July a fresh show is presented approximately every 5/6 weeks. Performances are on Fridays, Saturdays and Sundays, usually over two weekends. This allows the school to use the theatre during the week. Bryan continues to design for us, and his posters and publicity give us the professional presentation that has always been a feature of the Northern Theatre Company.

In 1988 I applied successfully for the post of Head of Drama at Wyke Sixth Form College. Quite a leap from the primary school teaching but one which I have enjoyed. Above all the move has increased my awareness of the needs of young people with regard to theatre and I made a positive decision to increase the Youth Theatre work.

Through the Northern Theatre Company School and through the Sixth Form College I have been fortunate in having some of the most talented youngsters in Hull to work with and I can say quite honestly that it has been my favourite time. It has been a rewarding experience and we have tackled together many classics and also original shows.

One of these, *Love Kevin*, was written with Thom Stridd, and Jonathan Holtby wrote the music. We entered it for the Lloyds Bank Challenge contest. The play tells the story of a young boy who leaves home and Hull to go up to London where he gets drawn into the rent-boy racket. It was based on the true story of a boy who came to the school. It caused a stir in Hull which I never quite understood. There was a highly moralistic attitude to the play that caused a controversy that I resented deeply. The local paper called for it to be banned. The *Daily Mirror* spoke in graphic terms of homosexual scenes with young boys although they had no basis for this whatsoever: they just made it up. This in turn attracted unsavoury paedophiles to the theatre — they left of course when they discovered there was nothing in it for them.

But the show was supported by the Principal of Wyke College and other influential spokespeople and it went ahead with Jody Crozier playing the part of Kevin. It was selected as one of the 12 shows out of 200 to be presented at the Royal National Theatre and we also took it to the Edinburgh Fringe where it was acclaimed and even made a profit on the box office — a rare occurrence in Edinburgh.

The following year, 1991, we did well again with a play called *Out of Mind*. It told the story of a boy with cerebral palsy and was based on the life of Ron Walker, a local disabled actor and theatre enthusiast. In the play the leading roles were taken by Anthony Hoggard, Andy Feeton and Samantha Hardcastle. Once more we were chosen to play at the National Theatre and this time BBC 2 included us in a documentary programme shown over two weeks at peak viewing time. Our company of young people rose to the occasion magnificently and I was very proud of them. Between us we really felt we'd put Hull on the map.

Sometimes I wonder if other people feel this way, though. In 1992 we received a body blow when the City Council reduced their financial assistance to the project and the County Council told us they could not support us with project funding this year. The Lincolnshire and Humberside Arts Association has never, so far, shown any interest in us, although things look more hopeful with the new Yorkshire Arts Board.

One problem is, I think, that we are difficult to define and place in a neat category. Yet we offer a professional support system *i.e.* myself as director and Bryan as designer. We put on productions with mixed professional and amateur casts, often of A Level texts that local students would be unable to see otherwise. We run a professionally staffed school. We run a Youth Theatre that is amongst the best in the country. We offer amateur groups in the City somewhere to perform. Quite a parcel!

So this concludes my brief story of the Northern Theatre Company. I'd just like to say a word about the future. My students have all got ambition to succeed. Many have gone on into professional theatre. I have now reached the age of 50 and I have found that ambition doesn't go away with age. In the last decade of the century I would like to see our productions achieving national recognition and Northern Theatre Youth becoming established as one of this country's top youth theatre companies.

The Hull Suffragettes — *Spring Street Women's Theatre Workshop, 1984*

The Chicken Factory — *The Company of Women*

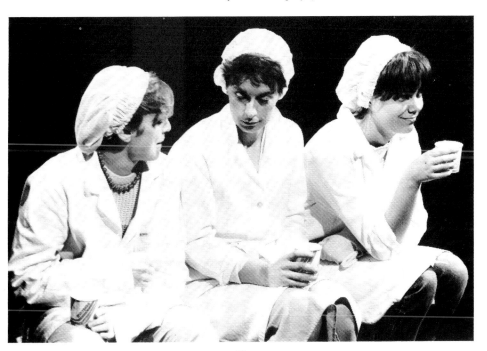

Out of Mind *at the Royal National Theatre. Left to right are Anna Gibbeson, Anthony Hoggard, Ian Mckellen, Jane Asher, Thom Stridd, Richard Green.*

*Richard Green as William Wilberforce.*

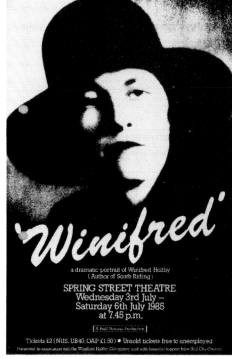

'*Winifred*'

a dramatic portrait of Winifred Holtby
( Author of South Riding )

SPRING STREET THEATRE
Wednesday 3rd July –
Saturday 6th July 1985
at 7.45 p.m.

A Hull Festival Production

Tickets £2 ( NUS, UB40, OAP £1.50) ● Unsold tickets free to unemployed

Presented in association with the Winifred Holtby Committee and with financial support from Hull City Council

90

*The cast of* Steeltown *the story of Scunthorpe's iron and steel industry, 1988.*

(*Photograph by courtesy of Dave Whatt*)

*Averil Coult and Rupert Creed.*     *Photograph by courtesy of Dave Whatt*

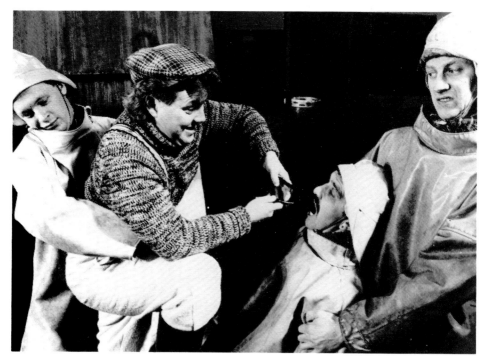

The Northern Trawl, 1985    *(Photograph by courtesy of Dave Whatt)*

Streetbeat, 1990.    *(Photograph by courtesy of Dave Whatt)*

A Day By the Sea: *Easington's village play was presented in the atmospheric setting of the 14th-century tithe barn in July, 1990.*

Reap the Whirlwind: *The Howden community play, 1988.*

*Gillian Holtby and Chris Lee working on costumes for the Hull City Play, 1992.*

*The first script development meeting of the Hull City Play.*

CHAPTER SEVEN

# REMOULD THEATRE COMPANY 1981-1992

## by Rupert Creed

### The First Year 81-82

Remould Theatre Company was founded in January, 1981, by Averil Coult and myself. 'Home grown' professional theatre was at that time in short supply: whilst there were two venues in Hull hosting touring theatre (Humberside Theatre and the New Theatre), the only company actually based in the county was Hull Truck, and in the early 80's Hull Truck was still essentially a touring outfit performing more often outside the region, particularly in London, than in the local area. Humberside Theatre in the 1970s had developed both an 'in-house' repertory company and a Theatre in Education Team but by 1981 financial constraints had led to these companies being disbanded, leaving the theatre functioning primarily as a touring venue.

So we could see the opportunity for a new company to start in the region, but there was also a purely personal reason: I had graduated with a degree in drama and German from Hull University in 1978 and wanted to follow a career in the theatre. I'd worked as a stage manager with Hull Truck and then for a further year as assistant director to Mike Bradwell with a bursary from the Arts Council, but, once that year was finished, it was a case of either going back to a stage management role or finding employment elsewhere. It was unlikely, given my lack of experience, that anyone would employ me as a writer or director, so the only way to get work would be to create it for myself. Averil had also worked with Hull Truck as publicity officer and had done freelance radio broadcasting and a variety of PR work so, with the balance of organisational experience on her side and the naivety and ambition on mine, and a simple shared desire to 'make something happen' we started Remould.

Why did we call the company Remould?. Firstly we wanted our plays to appeal to a broad-based audience, and like countless other companies before us such as North West Spanner, Belt and Braces, and indeed Hull Truck, we wanted a name that disassociated us from the traditional high culture image of theatre. There was always an artistic logic behind the name —

theatre draws on reality and moulds it into dramatic form — but until we started producing documentary plays in 1985 that was hardly applicable except in the most generalised sense, and. to be honest, I think we wanted to be seen less as 'artists' and more as 'workers'. Of course the inevitable happened: in the same way as Hull Truck used to receive enquires about removal services, we began to get phone calls from people wanting to buy tyres.

The second reason for the name is that very early on we had a phone call from the Arts Council. We had written to them a week or so beforehand enquiring about possible grants, but at the point when they rang up out of the blue we still hadn't made any firm decision about the company's name. When asked what it was, I fumbled frantically for the piece of paper with the shortest of possible names and failing to find it, confidently trotted out the only one I could remember — Remould.

The company policy was very simple: write a play and produce it. There was a commitment to providing a new theatre provision for the region but equally there was a desire to tour further afield and establish a wider reputation. At that time we certainly hadn't thought through the idea of what 'community theatre' could be. At the start we had very little in the way of resources. Averil's house was the company's base, her car was the only means of transport, and her home phone was the public point of contact. Apart from the letterheaded paper the company as such did not exist — it certainly had no formal legal basis — and of course there was little or no money. Our first play, *The Nuclear Cabaret*, was mounted on a grant of £350 from Lincolnshire and Humberside Arts which just about covered the production and publicity costs — nobody got paid. The actors and musicians were all local friends and acquaintances, some from the University Drama Department, others from David Whatt's local blues band, 'The Rialtos'. I wrote the play, Dave wrote the music, designed and built the set, and the whole thing was ferried to rehearsals on the roof rack of Averil's car. Outreach Community Arts provided free rehearsal space and Humberside Theatre provided the venue for the performance week at the end of April. Shortly before rehearsals began we had a phone call from Yorkshire Television who wanted extracts from the play to be the main feature of their regional arts programme, *Calendar Carousel*, fronted by Roy Castle. It all seemed a bit unlikely (why us, why an unknown theatre company?) but we gave the impression it was only what we were used to, and yes we were all Equity members (a lie — only two of us were), and yes we could discuss fees and contracts (we were actually going to get paid for it!). Some of the scenes were pre-recorded but the main part was performed live in front of a studio audience in Leeds on the morning of the day we premiered the play at Humberside Theatre, so we ended the night elated at our double first.

*The Nuclear Cabaret* was a musical satire on the nuclear arms race and the civil defence industry, and its success was no doubt due to its topicality. In 1981 Cruise missiles were arriving at Greenham, superpower politics were locked into increasingly absurd and obscene forms of nuclear war fighting strategies, and CND were experiencing a massive increase in membership as people took to the streets in protest. The first half of the play was a revue-format satire on attitudes to nuclear war and civil defence, and the second half followed the scenario of a group of nuclear war supervisors in Humberside. In retrospect, the play was no doubt simplistic in content and derivative in form, but it was relevant, accessible and entertaining theatre and it struck a resonant chord with audiences wherever we played.

The success of *The Nuclear Cabaret* in Hull encouraged us further. We decided to take the play to the Edinburgh Festival, and in order to raise funds to do this we wrote and produced the company's first children's play *The Black and White Rainbow* and also did a short tour of the North-East with *Nuclear Cabaret*. Outreach Community Arts had loaned us their van and, with the actors in a second hired van, we set off to Redcar. A few miles north of York the hired van broke down, and then on the return trip a few days later the front wheel came off at a roundabout — the first of many such problems we were to experience with vehicles on tour. We were fortunate to acquire our own touring van shortly before we set off for the Edinburgh Festival. It was a blue and white British Leyland van (the kind used by the Post Office in those days) and we converted it with extra seats for the actors in front and space behind for set and props. The van was donated by Alec Horsley of Northern Foods, a local benefactor, who over the years had played a crucial role in encouraging and providing much needed financial support to a wide variety of arts groups, organisations and causes. The van served us well for a number of years but shortage of funds meant that we could never afford to keep it serviced and maintained properly and from '83 onwards we were caught in a Catch 22 situation of investing ever larger sums of precious money into a vehicle that was past its best. But back in the summer of '81 there was a tremendous feeling of excitement in setting off to Edinburgh in our van with the Remould logo plastered on the side. *The Nuclear Cabaret* was a big success at the festival, playing three sell-out weeks to enthusiastic audiences and rave reviews, and on returning to Hull we were determined to make the company a long-term proposition.

The next production was *Passport to Pluto*, written by Dave Whatt and myself. It was conceived as an alternative adult Christmas entertainment and played at Humberside Theatre over Christmas, '81. The Hull-based plot centred around a second-hand spaceship purchased on Hessle Road by a dubious character called Dennis Tossa who under the name of 'Icarus Travel' is promoting weekend package tours around the solar system. The audience for the play were thus the package holiday- makers who were offered the delights of live in-flight cabaret entertainment as well as the educational sights of the solar system, or, as the publicity for the play described it, 'a fun-packed show full of sex, drugs and astronomy'.

In the spring of '82 we started our first proper national tour with *The Nuclear Cabaret*, which included five months of performances as far afield as Winchester in the south and Tain, to the north of Inverness. We played just about anywhere people would book us, and we ended up in some 'interesting' venues. High spots included post-show ceilidhs in Scotland and a level of hospitality from Highland promoters that was greatly appreciated at the time but began to take its toll of body and mind in the days following. Low spots included a sequence of gigs promoted by Students Union Ents officers. One such promotion at North Staffs Polytechnic involved us spending three hours on arrival trying to locate the person who had booked us, another three hours driving round with him knocking on people's doors to see if they were willing to put us up for the night, and the next morning another three hours trying to locate a suitable hall for us to perform in. The final straw came when five minutes before we were due to start the show there was no audience and very little likelihood of an audience and he came out with the comment, 'Do you fancy staying and doing the show tomorrow instead? John Cooper Clarke's on tonight. I could get you free tickets.' We drove home.

Because of the nature of the tour and the travelling distances involved it was impossible for the company to sign on and at that time we were all earning the princely sum of £30 a week. We could rarely afford to stay in bed and breakfasts, so accommodation was usually arranged with friends of the promoters; it could be good, bad or very bad. Sometimes it was non-existent. We did one performance at Ware in Hertfordshire where the promoter had completely forgotten to organise any accommodation. Just before the start of the second half she got up onstage and made an impassioned plea for members of the audience to come forward and offer an actor a bed for the night. She stressed how clean, polite and well-behaved we all were, and we half expected her to drag us out from the wings and line us up for our teeth to be inspected. The tour finished in May with three weeks in London at the Gate Theatre in Notting Hill, and, although exhausted, we felt pleased with what we had achieved in our first year: we'd written and produced three new plays, mounted a national tour, performed in London and Edinburgh and received enthusiastic reviews in the local and national press. The commitment and enthusiasm were there — but so was the lack of money.

**Plays and Money Problems 1982-1984**

In the autumn of 1982 the company attracted its first four-figure grant — £3,000 from Humberside County Council. Strictly speaking it wasn't a grant, but a fee, in return for which we had to provide a children's show to tour throughout the county for four weeks in January. Prior to this we'd received small grants from Lincolnshire and Humberside Arts and writing money from the Arts Council, but these amounts had hardly been enough to cover basic costs, leaving little or nothing to pay ourselves or our actors. For the first time we had a guaranteed sum of money with which to budget a production and tour and it marked the start of a funding commitment from the County Council which has continued to grow to this day. Averil and I co-wrote *Eric of the Round Table*, and, as the original pool of actors and musicians from *Cabaret* and *Pluto* had dispersed to other work or home commitments, we advertised nationally and held auditions for performers. Dave Whatt continued with the company as designer and set builder. Rehearsals began in December, with the play touring throughout January. The touring schedule was all local but involved two and sometimes three shows a day, which, together with travel and fit-up times, meant some very long working days. A typical sequence would involve travelling early in the morning to Immingham and doing fit-up, performing in the afternoon and evening, packing it all in the van, travelling to Cleethorpes, getting it all out and setting it all up again, and then travelling back to Hull at two in the morning and setting off again at 8.00 am ready for a 10.00 am show back in Cleethorpes. Because of the towns we played at — Immingham, Scunthorpe, Goole, Grimsby etc. — we dubbed it the 'Monto Carlo' tour and I think for some actors, particularly those from London, it came as a bit of a culture shock. *Eric* proved to be very successful and the acting company worked well together, so towards the end of the tour Averil and I put forward a plan that would involve the actors becoming in effect a permanent company throughout 1983.

Throughout the spring and early summer we toured *Eric* nationally and in the gaps got involved in a bizarre variety of fund-raising ventures, including performance events for Chaplins restaurant, Hull City Football Club, and a local tyre company. One of the actors, Robert Sim, got his name into the Guinness Book of Records by singing non-stop for a week at the Waterfront Club.

The company were also involved in the Hull Pageant that spring which re-enacted the refusal of entry into the city to Charles I in 1642. The Saturday evening before the main event, the actors in two separate groups went round the old town pubs, lobbying for allegiance either to the King or Parliament. Licence extensions had been granted and the pubs were crammed with weekend drinkers and the actors dressed in full period costume would get up on the tables and give a series of rabble-rousing speeches which drew a highly authentic response — a near riot. A recurring problem was the curiosity expresses by some of the women as to what the actor was wearing 'under his skirt' and the problem was compounded by the fact that the actors were being paid in kind with copious amounts of free alcohol at each pub. The pageant on the Sunday drew a massive crowd and gave us some interesting moments — the actor playing King Charles had to ride down

Whitefriargate followed by a regiment of the Sealed Knot and then to perform the scene in front of the town gate on horseback. He'd never ridden before, and the only chance he had to try it out was during the actual performance. Another actor had to be executed at the end of the event, and the beheading was to be carried out by one of the Sealed Knot members, who are quite enthusiastic about that sort of thing and like them to look authentic. We were told it would involve an axe (presumably false) and a special contraption designed to produce the maximum gory effect. Again the first time the actor had the chance to try it out was during the actual performance. As he placed his head on the block his confidence was not increased by the executioner whispering to him, 'I think it's safe but if it does go wrong it won't matter will it — 'cos it's a one-off event.'

Despite the increase in touring and the income from fund raising events we still hadn't enough money to produce the adult play *Exit the Lemming*, and take it and *Eric* to the Edinburgh Festival, so we were forced to take out a bank loan. Averil's house was put on the line as security. It was a serious personal risk but we were already committed to the programme and backing out at that stage would have involved heavy financial penalties. It was a gamble and it didn't pay off. Playing at Edinburgh that year nearly bankrupted us personally and the company came very close to folding. When you take a show to the Festival its essential you pay for the privilege of working. Normally the company would be paid a fee by a theatre for each show, but at Edinburgh the situation is reversed: you pay the venue-promoter, and in 1983 it was costing us around £3000 for two performance slots a day over the three-week run. In addition to this are the publicity costs, accommodation (rented accommodation is in great demand and consequently expensive) and of course all the production costs involved in a new show. So, even if you are operating on a profit-share basis with the company members (i.e, no guaranteed wages), the financial investment is still considerable. So is the pressure to get an audience, and competition for audiences at the Festival is intense. The schedule was too much — *Eric* at 10 am, *Lemming* at 8 pm, with only about 15 minutes turn-round time between shows that were on before and after, and the afternoon spent mainly on the streets doing publicity stunts or simply leafleting. The 12-hour days continued for three weeks with only the one day off in the entire period.

*Eric* did well, but *Exit the Lemming* got bad-to-indifferent reviews and played to very small audiences. Everybody worked extremely hard but, it seemed, the more effort we put in, the less tangible the reward, and the tensions inevitably rose as people became more tired over the period and were unable to live off the small amount we were paying ourselves. Day by day we were working ourselves into debt and it was a relief for the Festival to be over. To curtail costs we decided not to hire a second van as we had done on the way up, so on the final day of performance Averil and myself drove the company van back to Hull with the *Eric* set, unloaded it, got a few hours sleep and then set off to Edinburgh to pick up the actors and load the *Lemming* set.

We had a full touring programme lined up for the autumn and this offered the only means for the company to pay off its debts, but it also meant that the actors had to continue on minimal wages when we had all anticipated that the hard work of the first half of the year would bring a reasonable wage by the autumn. Everybody was in dire financial straits and some wanted to leave but in the event everybody honoured their commitment and saw the tour through. The van was driven back from Edinburgh but then broke down again almost instantly and it became apparent the replacement engine was little better then the original one. Fortunately a friend located yet another engine and fitted it for us free of charge, but on tour there was the constant worry of breakdown and the thing was really only going on a wing and a prayer. On one occasion the driver's door was opened and the wind blew it straight off and down the road. One high point in an otherwise difficult period was a week at the Melkweg in Amsterdam, our first performance abroad.

The tour finished in November and some actors opted to stay on for the Christmas show — a remounting of *The Black and White Rainbow*. The company was getting back on to a reasonable financial footing and the threat of Averil losing her house was receding, but then a week or so into rehearsals we were hit from an unexpected quarter — the Department of Health and Social Security. Over the previous three years we had by necessity been signing on the dole between touring periods but, once on tour, we signed off even though we were hardly earning enough to live on. There were of course grey areas - it could be argued that the work I was doing personally in writing or co-writing the plays and helping set up the tours meant that I was technically 'unavailable for work' or 'not actively seeking employment' during those times, but as a large percentage of actors, writers and theatre directors are forced by necessity to create their own work opportunities in this way (most of the London fringe theatre works on that basis) we felt we were not acting dishonestly — quite the opposite. We felt justified that we were making a serious effort to create work for ourselves and others in a time of high un-employment. Ironically a few years later the government started offering quite substantial grants for people to start up companies, and many individual artists and newly-formed theatre groups benefited from this, but in late '83 the opposite seemed to be the case. The DHSS were of the opinion that what we were doing constituted a potential serious fraud. Myself, previous and current company members were rigorously investigated by the DHSS and at times it felt distinctly intimidating. It wasn't quite the 'dawn-raid' syndrome but it felt uncomfortably close: a DHSS officer would turn up on the doorstep early in the morning requiring certain details to be clarified, prefaced by the warning that what we said could be used in evidence in court. Up to this point the company's financial transactions had been kept informally but the threat of prosecution prompted us to have the books audited by a professional accountant. We subsequently learnt a DHSS officer had used his powers of access and spent several days in the accountant's office going through the books and receipts personally. It all seemed incredibly overblown and it dragged on for months. Finally it was resolved to the satisfaction of the DHSS — no major fraud was unearthed but they did decide that a couple of actors had received benefit that technically covered a few of the days at some point of the tour. The amount involved a few pounds, which were paid back and that was that. In retrospect, the whole investigation was fairly trivial, but at that time it caused a lot of anxiety and pressure to all involved.

At the end of the Black and White Rainbow tour in Spring '84, Averil and I reassessed the whole situation. We'd learnt from the previous year that we'd financially and physically over-stretched ourselves and our actors, and that, if we were to continue, the tour would have to be planned further in advance, budgeted more realistically, and be of a specific duration to maximise income over the period and thereby generate as much available money as possible with which to pay company members. The real problem of course was the lack of funding — we were trying to run a professional company on next to nothing and after three and a half years of hard work we seemed to be no nearer to securing even the most basic level of funding from organisations such as Lincolnshire & Humberside Arts or the Arts Council. That year saw the start of closer funding partnerships between Humberside County Council and the LHA, and Alun Bond, LHA's drama officer, together with Andrew Dixon, who had recently been appointed as the county's first arts officer, worked hard to secure project and touring funding for the company. Wages were still low by anybody's estimate (I think we'd gone up to the dizzy heights of about £60 a week) but it was a guaranteed wage throughout the rehearsal and touring period and it meant that nobody was actually worse off financially at the end. That year also saw us move into our own rehearsal and office space on Lowgate, in a former music hall theatre that Hull City Council made available to the company on a peppercorn rent. It was cold and to a visitor probably unattractive (faded second-hand carpets and junk-shop furniture was all we could afford) but the building had great character and atmosphere and the necessary space for rehearsal, set-building, storage and offices. The company now had a base and the days of hassling for somewhere to rehearse, and shifting bits of set from one house to another, were thankfully gone for good.

Village hall touring was a new and rewarding experience and we began to build a substantial audience following in rural communities in all parts of the region. Performing in a village hall reveals some interesting aspects about the nature of a theatre event. Firstly, the hall is not designed primarily for performing plays: there is no backstage, dressing rooms, or theatre lights. Secondly, the hall is used by the community for a wide range of activities of which a play performance is usually only a small part — it is their space, it is 'owned' by the audience. Thirdly, a performance at a village hall usually involves an audience that constitutes a substantial number or at least a representative cross-section of that whole village (and this is assisted by the fact that usually the 'promoter' is not a paid professional but simply a member of that community who is helping to organise the event and sell the tickets).

All these factors combine to alter subtly the traditional relationship between the professional actor (and the play as a whole) and an audience: the actor is not on 'home' territory; there is no room for preciousness or preconceived notions of professional status; he can rely neither on theatre technology nor the aura of the space to cover any shortcomings in his performance of the play. On the other side are the audience who in the main are not regular theatre-goers and do not share assumptions about how an audience should behave: they are not 'knowing' about theatre and because there is often a broad cross-section of age, class and attitudes their response to a play is quite a testing one. It will certainly expose the writer's preconceptions or assumptions. All these factors help brush aside some of the trivial paraphernalia of theatre and bring it back to the essential connection between performer and audience. There is a danger in oversimplifying all of this — a purpose-built theatre has many technical advantages impossible to re-create in the restrictions of a village hall, and there are equally many theatres in the country which attract a very diverse audience. There is also the complex issue of whether or not a play is suitable for a village hall audience and what exactly does 'suitable' mean?. The first Remould shows that toured on the village hall circuit were children's plays (but written with adult enjoyment in mind as well!) and as such were very much in demand as family Christmas shows, but as yet we hadn't confronted the idea of touring more 'demanding' or 'serious' plays to village halls. At that time our understanding of community theatre meant simply 'reaching the parts other theatre companies don't reach'.

### Documentary Plays 1985-1987

1985 was a turning point in the history of the company. It was the year Remould became a properly constituted company and a registered educational charity with a formal board structure; it was the year we secured project funding from LHA and Humberside County Council and won our first major grant from the Arts Council; and it was the year of our first documentary oral history play, *The Northern Trawl*. Up to this point the company's work had been geared for both regional and national touring. We had developed our community touring within Humberside and Lincolnshire and at the same time aimed for artistic standards that would justify a national touring role, and we wanted to maintain this dual touring policy. But something was nagging us: were we really fulfilling the 'regional' role, simply by virtue of touring to a mix of local theatres and non-theatre venues such as community centres and village halls?. It was obvious that we needed in some way to develop our work so it would have a deeper connection with local audiences beyond that of simply turning up and 'doing a show', and it was through 'oral history' plays that we first found a way of achieving that objective.

The Northern Trawl was a play about Hull and Grimsby's deep-sea fishing industry, a subject obviously of specific relevance to the area, but more importantly it was based on the experiences of the trawlermen themselves: it was their story, told in their own words. We spent four months tape-recording their experiences and stories, and those of their wives and families, and built up an archive of recorded material that gave a first-hand witness account of the rise and demise of the industry, what the work involved, and what these people had seen and lived through. The play was then based entirely on these reminiscences presenting an accurate, authentic and heartfelt portrayal of the industry and the Hessle Road community. Local trawlermen sat in on our rehearsals to advise and correct where necessary and in October we started a five week regional tour in a hired vehicle (the Remould van had failed its MOT and was sold to two Moroccan tumblers from Birmingham who were in Hull with a travelling circus). The response to the Northern Trawl was overwhelming from audiences and critics alike, and when the show played in Hull, Spring Street Theatre was packed with trawlermen and their families, many of whom had never set foot in a theatre before — they certainly weren't regular theatre-goers. During performances there would be a constant commentary of recognition and approval and a total sense of identification with what was being presented onstage. This was particularly poignant in a scene which described the loss of three ships in 1968 — a tragedy which at the time deeply affected the entire Hessle Road fishing community: 17 years on, families, friends and relatives in the audience held hands and wept as the incident was retold and the memories re-lived. As Robin Thornber, writing of the play in The Guardian, put it: 'It does what theatre should, it makes you laugh, cry and think.' In the bar after the show trawlermen would regale us with further experiences and anecdotes and the common overall response was that their story, the story of the fishing industry, was one that needed to be told and that with The Northern Trawl we had got it absolutely right. What in effect they were expressing was a sense of 'ownership' of the play — in the narrow materialistic sense, but in the wider sense that the play was a shared expression of their history, their lives and their feelings. It was clear to us that it was the oral history process of creating the play that had made this possible. The concept of 'ownership' was one that became increasingly important in Remould's work and a few years later we were to develop this further through community plays.

103

Two days after the first *Northern Trawl* tour finished we started rehearsals for the new children's show, *The Time Travellers of Transylvania*, for which we had secured our first Arts Council project grant. Averil and I had started to co-write the play but time was against us so we commissioned Andy Andrews to complete the script during rehearsals.

In 1986 we consolidated the company's work, touring nationally in the spring and autumn with *The Northern Trawl* including dates at the Cleethorpes and Beverley Folk Festivals. In between we launched our first programme of summer work involving performances and workshops designed primarily for children throughout the county. *The Northern Trawl* was recorded for radio (the first of many subsequent projects in association with BBC Radio Humberside), a record of the music by John Conolly and Bill Meek was released, and the script of the play was published. Robert Hewison, a London arts correspondent, spent a few days with the company on tour and wrote an article for the Sunday Times describing Remould as 'the national theatre that travels to you'. Our vehicle problems were finally resolved with the County Council providing a brand new Mercedes van for the company.

That autumn we commissioned Mary Cooper to co-write a new oral history play, *Close to the Bone*, which examined the world of nursing. Whilst research was progressing, we rehearsed a new children's play, *The Battle for Bucket Manor*, which toured regionally and nationally from December 1986 through to March, 1987. Both plays attracted funding from the Arts Council, LHA and Humberside County Council. *Close to the Bone* involved not only tape-recording the stories and experiences of local nurses, but also observing their work on the wards at Hull Royal Infirmary. A large modern hospital has many separate disciplines and functions and the research involved long hours on intensive care, orthopaedic, geriatric and children's wards, and several night shifts on casualty. At times it felt uncomfortably close to voyeurism but we always respected the wishes of both patients and staff and took our responsibilities concerning the confidentiality of the material seriously. As the trust was built up between us the staff and the patients, we became privy to increasingly touching and at times emotionally distressing situations. The experience was invaluable for it exposed us not only to the anxiety and vulnerability that the patient is experiencing but also the emotional burden taken on by nurses in the course of their work. It taught us first hand that nursing is as much about caring for a person as treating the medically ill. And of course it wasn't all sadness and sorrow: there's a lot of humour in nursing and that came through in the play as well.

Rehearsals for *Close to the Bone* started mid-February, 1987, and as with *The Northern Trawl* the job for the actors was not just the traditional one of learning lines, rehearsing scenes etc, but also in effect taking a crash course in the profession that the play is portraying. Actors seem to relish the challenge of these documentary plays, for it means that their work as performers requires them to refer constantly back to a very concrete reality, whether it's to do with the technical detail of the work they are portraying, the procedures involved, or the emotional experience that the original person who told the story is going through. Because of this, the actors in these plays rarely seem to have the traditional problem of 'what's my character's motivation?.' Set against this is the enemy of time. *Close to the Bone* was only partly pre-scripted (my fault, not Mary's), most of it being written and then re-worked during rehearsals. Helen Porter had composed some highly effective four-part harmony a capella music for the play and required more time to rehearse than I'd anticipated: this, together with the process of scene drafts being re-worked with the actors, meant that rehearsals began to feel like a race against time. In retrospect it was a very creative rehearsal period and the collective tensions were all positive ones and ultimately benefited the final play, but at the time I felt I was in a constant state of barely-controlled panic. The play opened in Boston, Lincolnshire, in mid-March and toured regionally and nationally, culminating in a successful three-week run in June as the Croydon Warehouse Theatre in south London. The play was recorded for radio, nominated for the Sony National Radio Awards, and drew an enthusiastic response from audiences and critics up and down the country. The Times described it as 'deft and enthralling' and the Nursing standard stated it was 'Possibly the best portrayal of nursing and nurses ever.' We felt, as with *The Northern Trawl*, that we had achieved what we had set out to do: the play had special relevance for and relationship with the people whose profession it was portraying and at the same time was an entertaining, informative and compelling piece of theatre for a general audience.

## Howden Community Play 1987-1988

Whilst *Close to the Bone* was on tour we began work on a large scale community play for Howden, a rural market town in Humberside. The impetus for the project came from a number of sources. We had performed many times at Howden and the promoting group, Howdenshire Live Arts, had requested that we undertake a project, such as a series of workshops or a residency, that would provide more than a one-off theatre performance. At the same time we went to see a community play in Gainsborough directed by Jon Oram who was at that time director of Colway Theatre Trust, the organisation that under the original direction of Ann Jellicoe had pioneered the concept of community plays in the south-west of England. This in turn led to Averil and myself participating in a community play training course run by Colway which, in turn, led us to propose a community play for Howden. With oral history plays we had found a means of involving the community directly in the creation of professional theatre — in effect the community provides the material for the play which is then rehearsed and performed by a group of professional actors. But a community play takes the ethos of community involvement to its logical limit — the play is researched within a community, its subject matter is drawn from the community's past and/or present, and the whole community assists in all aspects of organising and mounting the final production. The projects involve a small core of professional theatres workers but the play itself is performed by a cast of entirely local people.

In the spring of 1987 we established a group of local people in Howden who began researching all aspects of the town's history. At this stage we had no idea what the play's focus would be and it wasn't until early summer that the story of Snowdon Dunhill began to emerge as a prime contender. Dunhill was a local corn thief who had gained a reputation as the 'Howden Highwayman', and in the early 19th century a small book had been published detailing his life and exploits. He, and most of his extended family, were tried at various points for their crimes, and transported to Australia. The research team began an intensive study authenticating the incidents described in the book and this in turn uncovered the story of the Clarkson family, in particular that of Bernard Clarkson who was a prominent landowner, banker and Methodist preacher. It was largely through his initiative that Dunhill was brought to trial, but the Clarkson family in turn suffered misfortune. Through imprudent land purchase they over-stretched themselves financially, their bank collapsed and Bernard ironically ended up his days, like Dunhill, in Australia. As we pieced the facts together a fascinating story emerged of two families, one rich and one poor, locked in a conflict that brought them mutual downfall and divided their local community.

Whilst the research for the play was progressing we established a core steering group of local people, held a public meeting to launch the project and in the autumn began an intensive series of workshops in drama, dance, music and mask-making. Other teams were established for fund-raising, set-building, publicity and box-office and a series of events took place that drew in ever larger numbers of participants in the overall project.

Casting for *Reap the Whirlwind* began in December. We had set ourselves a ground rule that the play was open to anyone regardless of age or previous acting experience and that every person in the play would have a named character part. I had begun writing the play envisaging a cast size of around 100, but over 130 people turned up for casting, so new characters were created and the play revised accordingly. Casting for a community play is a lengthy process: the majority of the performers have home and work commitments and rehearsals have to be planned taking into consideration the time that people are able or willing to commit, so we drew up large charts of individuals' availability for rehearsals.

Rehearsals began in January and as the opening night drew closer the level of activity, enthusiasm and sheer commitment on all sides went way beyond our expectations. There was a genuine sense of a community drawing together to give, help and support each other in creating a unique and unforgettable experience. The school hall where the promenade performance was to take place was transformed with multiple stages and scaffolding and a massive light and sound rig, and on the opening night in March I think the audience was astonished at what the community had achieved.

After the first night the two weeks of performances sold out within a day, and we had to disappoint large numbers of people who had left it too late to book. The play was subsequently recorded for radio with a slightly pared down cast (the full cast wouldn't have physically fitted in the studio!) and we held a series of follow-up public meetings in Howden for local people to discuss and formulate the shape of future arts activities in their community. Over 300 local people had been directly involved in the project and this enthusiasm and active involvement in the arts continues in Howden to this day. A community play not only gives people the enjoyment and satisfaction of being part of a large exciting theatre event but in a wider sense it empowers them — it increases individuals' confidence, it encourages communication and trust, and generates friendships, and people learn to confront problems and solve them together: 'community' goes beyond being just a descriptive label and becomes an active shared experience. This can only happen if the community are genuinely involved, if their input is encouraged and then respected, if they are allowed to take 'ownership' of what is after all their play. The effort and skills of the professional co-ordinating team in this respect are crucial but more important is their attitude: plays are not the preserve of professionals — theatre can be with people, not simply for them.

Throughout this time the company was still operating on project funding and although this had risen substantially, it still meant we were having to commit ourselves to a programme of work a long way in advance without the guarantee that the money would be there for us to carry it out. In addition to the new area of work we were developing in Howden, we were maintaining a programme of participatory drama work over the summer and a high level of regional and national touring with both the children's shows and the adult documentary plays. We had only three permanent company members — myself, Averil and an assistant administrator — and the administrative workload had increased considerably over the years. We felt that if we were to continue and develop our work effectively, the company had to be funded on a regular basis, and that year we secured a three year funding franchise from LHA that would come into effect from April 1988, together with an annual revenue funding commitment from the County Council. Our future programme of work would focus on the oral history plays, developing the community play projects and establishing a new post of a community drama worker with a brief to extend the outreach and education work of the company. With the increase of work in these areas we felt it was unrealistic to continue touring the children's plays so with some regret both from our side and our audiences, the *Pirates of Atlantis* tour that autumn was the last Remould children's show.

### *Steeltown* and *The Care Takers* 1988-1989

In May 1988 we started researching our third oral history play — Steeltown, the story of Scunthorpe's iron and steel industry. Scunthorpe Borough Council had commissioned the play and, drawing on our experience in Howden, we established a research team of local people including working and retired steelworkers both to assist on the tape-recorded interviews and gather as much historical, technical and photographic material as possible. British Steel gave their full co-operation to the project, allowing us access to their film and photographic archive, and organising trips for us round the steelworks so we could see at first hands the methods of contemporary steelmaking. We were overawed by the sheer heat and scale of the process and despite the fact that the play was to tour to our usual circuit of small-scale venues, we were determined from the outset that it should convey the visual spectacle of steelmaking: Dave Whatt managed the near-impossible task of designing a steel works for the stage with a blast furnace, steel furnace and rolling mill, and still got the whole thing to fit in the back of the van.

The play premièred at Scunthorpe Civic Theatre in October to an enthusiastic local audience containing many families whose members spanned several generations of steelworkers. The music composed by Roger Watson was released as a cassette, the play was recorded for radio, and a successful six month tour took in steel communities in Scotland, Wales and the north-east. An encouraging sign of the company's growing national reputation was the way the documentary plays were both attracting and sustaining audiences regardless of whether or not the town, village or city we were performing in had a direct connection with the play's subject matter. Our community drama work in the region that year included a six week summer programme for children and young people, a Steeltown workshop programme for schools, a reminiscence project with the elderly members of a day centre in Grimsby, and a community project on Orchard Park Estate in Hull. That year Remould was one of only two theatre companies in the country to achieve full revenue-funding status from the Arts Council, on a three year franchise to start the following year. The decision meant that now all three of our main funding partners were committed to the company's long-term programme of work both in the region and nationally.

In 1989 we mounted our fourth oral history play, *The Care Takers*, which focused on the world of social work. The play was researched in close collaboration with Humberside Social Services who gave us access to a wide range of social work establishments and teams, also provided part-funding for the project. Initially this caused some controversy when a local councillor, who disagreed with the majority decision of the Social Services committee to offer the grant, decided to take his objections to the local press and radio. We were duly branded as a 'left-wing theatre company' which by virtue of receiving the grant was depriving elderly people of their home-helps, and the issue continued to smoulder up to the local May elections of that year, after which point it died away. The play with original music by Hilary Gordon opened that October, toured for six months, and attracted an enthusiastic response from audiences and critics. The play was recorded as a training video for Humberside Social Services and was produced as a radio play by BBC Radio Humberside and broadcast by other local radio stations up and down the country. We continued to develop our community drama work with our regular programme expanding to include week-long residencies in schools, with the community drama worker and the actors from *The Care Takers* working together with the pupils to devise a performance piece based on the young people's own experiences.

### *A Day by the Sea* and *Streetbeat* 1990-91

1990 was a busy year for the company. *The Care Takers* continued touring to March, and in May we remounted *Steeltown* as part of Scunthorpes Centenary of Steel Festival, with additional performances including the twin town of Lüneburg in West Germany. In addition the book of *Steeltown* was published, based in the reminiscence material gathered for the play, together with many previously unpublished photographs of the industry. From the beginning of the year we were also busy in Easington, a small village on the east coast of Humberside, working on a community play to be performed as part of the village's octo-centenary celebrations of the founding of the local church. We commissioned Sheila Yeger to write the play and *A Day by the Sea* was performed in July in the highly atmospheric setting of the village's 14th-century tithe barn. Easington has little more than 500 people on its electoral roll and, with a cast of around 70 local people and with many more involved in the research and the organisational and backstage work, we felt pleased that we had met the challenge of producing a community play in a small rural village.

In addition to all this we were busy researching our new documentary play, *Street Beat*, based on the work of Humberside Police. From April through to July co-writer Peter Spafford and myself accompanied police officers on the beat, both walking and in cars, and spent many hours of research with officers in various departments, including CID, plain-clothes, traffic, the Underwater Search unit and the mounted police and dog-handlers. It was a rather fascinating, eye-opening experience, and the project represented a unique collaboration between a police force and a theatre company. Police officers sat in on rehearsals, did improvisations with the actors and taught them many aspects of practical policing including physical restraint techniques and the intricacies of legal procedures. Policing is a highly contentious subject and from the outset we had made our position clear — that we intended to produce a realistic, honest, 'warts and all' portrayal of the bobby on the beat. The level of co-operation and trust from the police was extremely high: access was allowed to many areas that we hadn't anticipated and throughout the project there was no attempt to influence the outcome of the final play, either in the areas that it focused on or the image of the police it presented.

*Street Beat* premièred at Spring Street Theatre in October 1990. Opening nights are unique events with this kind of plays, for the audience contains a high percentage of the people who have been directly involved in the research. It is their stories and experiences being re-enacted before them, and that can be quite nerve-wracking for the actors who not only are performing the play for the first time publicly, but also to an audience whose personal response may be volatile and unpredictable (but hopefully appreciative). Add to this the contentiousness of the subject and the fact that on this occasion the 200 plus audience was almost entirely made up of police officers who by virtue of their job have a fairly commanding presence and physique. It all made for a very interesting first night. The play was a great success, not just with the police officers who enjoyed and identified with the actors' portrayal of their world, but also as we learnt on subsequent nights, with a more general audience who on the whole felt that the play did confront the issues and concerns that they as a members of the public have concerning the police. People have strong feelings about the subject, whether they are police officers on the one side or members of the public on the other, and perceptions from either side may be prejudiced or valid, and the challenge for us in doing the play was that, at the point of performance, police-public relationship is made literal and concrete by virtue of the public nature of the theatre event. In the opening scene, the houselights stay up and the actors as police officers come on one by one, and literally eye up the audience as if in a real public situation, and the analogy continues throughout the evening: we the audience, the general public, are presented or 'confronted' with the statements, opinions, and experiences of actual police officers through the filter of the actors, and how we respond to that, is all part of what the play is examining, relevant and provocative.

### Ten Years On — 1991

1991 marked the tenth anniversary of Remould and, together with the obvious desire to celebrate with a boisterous public party, it offered the chance to take stock of what we'd achieved and what we wanted to do in the future. We wanted to continue our policy of researching, writing and touring documentary plays, initiating and co-ordinating community plays in the region, and developing further outreach work through the post of Community Drama Worker. We had developed these three strands of work in our own particular way that we felt offered an effective and imaginative programme of community theatre work: community touring meant that we were taking theatre to areas that had little or no theatre provision; the 'oral history' plays were a method of actively involving the community in the creation of plays whilst at the same time producing theatre that connected with audiences in both theatres and community venues; the community plays took the process of community involvement to its logical conclusion; and the drama worker post could develop outreach work either on a separate project basis or linked with the documentary and community plays.

We decided in 1991 to produce a documentary play about our own profession — the theatre!. Maybe it was because it was the company's tenth anniversary, or maybe it was simply because we wanted to produce a play that we felt we could have a bit more licence and fun with — either way we decided to do *Making Faces*, an oral history play about actors.

There is an paradox in doing a realistic play about people whose job is to pretend and be someone else that night, and this led to writing a different kind of play from the previous documentaries. Most of the tape-recorded material was not issued in a verbatim way but was incorporated in the wholly invented story of an imaginary theatre company called Rollercoaster doing a touring production of Isben's *Ghosts*. So, the play had more of a traditional feel in that it had rounded characters and a fully developed story but with several overlapping layers of reality that deliberately get mixed up. It's an impossible play to describe — it was very funny and I think very honest about the nature of the profession. It was certainly a strange experience to be doing a play about doing a play and it required a level of distancing for all concerned for it not to become 'knowing' or self-indulgent.

## 1992

At the time of writing we are busy working on a community play for Hull which will be performed in June, 1992, as part of Hull Festival. Having done a community play in a small market town and then a village it is an interesting challenge to be doing one in a city. All community plays require the writer to ask what exactly is a community, and what is particular about this community — and the city is really a collection of smaller different communities that may or may not have a sense of a shared history or culture. There is the problem of scale: once a cast size rises above 200, certainly 300, it becomes very hard for the writer, director and the professional team to know people on an individual basis and their commitment and personal investment is either not generated or acknowledged — there is the danger that their involvement is merely as 'crowd fodder' in the play. There is also the question of time and resources and what approach is most suitable — you could easily do separate community plays for West, East, North Hull or indeed on any one of the estates, each of which would be equally valid. There is no 'right' answer to these questions but we have set ourselves some guide-lines for the project: it is a play about the City as a whole rather than part of a city; it will be performed in a large central location, City Hall; the cast of local people should be drawn from all parts of the City and represent a broad cross-section of age and social background; the subject of the play should be drawn from Hull's history and/or contemporary life, and as broad a cross-section of local people as possible and both responding to and stimulating their input into the script.

The research team have been working on the project since May, 1991, and as well as gathering a mountain of documentary material, have also been involved in tape-recording the reminiscences of Hull people. An attitude that came through strongly from the start was that the play should not focus on famous figures but should be about 'ordinary' Hull people — there was also a strong desire for a focus on the last century and humour!. Throughout the autumn and continuing into the spring there have been a series of workshops in drama, design, costume, dance and music taking place in North, East and the centre of Hull which have drawn in ever larger numbers of local people.

Jon Oram has been commissioned to both write and co-direct the Hull City Play and it is interesting working with a person who not only is very experienced at community plays but also is keen to develop their potential further. The celebratory aspect of community plays is of prime importance but with it comes a need to define or question what it is we are celebrating. There is limited value in producing a play with the people of Hull which in effect offers little more than mutual congratulation, but at the opposite end of the spectrum there would be no point in asking local people to be involved in a play that simply criticises or chastises them as its subject. The community play process itself must encourage this kind of debate and find positive ways in which these issues can be aired and fed back into the play. The process thus becomes an honest active experience of 'community' rather than simply an exercise in 'papering over the cracks', and in this way we all genuinely earn our celebration.

In the ten years since Remould began, the company has produced 16 new plays, mounted over 20 national and regional tours, and performed in over 300 different venues. We have gone from nothing but an idea and a name to a company with secure and substantial funding, a proven track record, and a loyal and ever growing audience following. Our work connects us with people from many different backgrounds and in many different ways. Through experience we have come to a clearer understanding of what we want to achieve and how to achieve it. Alan Plater once said words to the effect that theatres and theatre companies ought to fold after ten years because they tend to become stale and institutionalised and by continuing to soak up precious arts subsidy prevent new and more creative groups from starting, but I think we've got a few more creative years ahead of us yet.

*During 1992 Hull's history and heritage, contemporary culture and links with Europe have been the focus of the Hull Festival and many of the people mentioned in these chapters have taken part in the seven-month-long celebrations.*

*One of the main theatrical events, as described by Rupert Creed in the final chapter was the City play,* Vital Spark. *In Jon Oram's script the portrayals of the 1911 dockers' strike and the trawler disasters of 1968 were moving and forceful reminders of the heroism of the individuals involved. The theme of Noah's flood which ran throughout the play reminded me of the beginning of this book and the idea of a centre for the arts in a City church and how then, and in our medieval past, community theatre in Hull began with the Hull shipwrights'* Play of Noah. *For some of us the community play was a culmination of everything that theatre in the community stands for but for most it was a new beginning, with everyone talking about what is to happen next. Perhaps these essays can contribute to the deliberations?*

*Editor*